MW01136625

A.P. GIANNINI
THE PEOPLE'S BANKER

Francesca Valente

THE **M**
MENTORIS
PROJECT

The author has made every effort to ensure the accuracy of the information within this book was correct at time of publication. The author does not assume and hereby disclaims any liability to any party for any loss, damage, or disruption caused by errors or omissions, whether such errors or omissions result from accident, negligence, or any other cause.

Barbera Foundation, Inc.
P.O. Box 1019
Temple City, CA 91780

Copyright © 2017 Barbera Foundation, Inc.
Cover photo: Courtesy Call Bulletin Library, May 23, 1947, San Francisco History
              Room, Public Library—Civic Center, San Francisco California 94102
Cover design: Suzanne Turpin

More information at www.mentorisproject.org

ISBN: 978-1-947431-04-1

Library of Congress Control Number: 2017956761

All net proceeds from the sale of this book will be donated to Barbera Foundation, Inc. whose mission is to support educational initiatives that foster an appreciation of history and culture to encourage and inspire young people to create a stronger future.

The Mentoris Project is a series of novels and biographies about the lives of great Italians and Italian-Americans: men and women who have changed history through their contributions as scientists, inventors, explorers, thinkers, and creators. The Barbera Foundation sponsors this series in the hope that, like a mentor, each book will inspire the reader to discover how she or he can make a positive contribution to society.

Contents

Foreword   i

Chapter One: A Challenging Childhood   1

Chapter Two: Lorenzo Scatena:
          A New Role Model at the Waterfront   7

Chapter Three: The Founding of the Bank of Italy   23

Chapter Four: The Earthquake: Disaster and Opportunity   37

Chapter Five: The Dawn of Branch Banking   51

Chapter Six: Los Angeles: An Opportunity Not
          to be Missed   63

Chapter Seven: The Largest Bank West of Chicago   71

Chapter Eight: Celebrating Twenty Years of
          Tenacious Expansion   81

Chapter Nine: Fulfilling Dreams   93

Chapter Ten: Nationwide Banking: A Life-long Mission   105

Chapter Eleven: Betrayal from Within   115

Chapter Twelve: Return to the Battlefield   131

Chapter Thirteen: Back to the Good Times   143

Chapter Fourteen: Under Siege Again   147

Chapter Fifteen: The New Heart of the Bank of America   167

Chapter Sixteen: Giannini's Legacy   183

Epilogue   187

Notes   197

About the Author   204

Foreword

First and foremost, Mentor was a person. We tend to think of the word *mentor* as a noun (a mentor) or a verb (to mentor), but there is a very human dimension embedded in the term. Mentor appears in Homer's *Odyssey* as the old friend entrusted to care for Odysseus's household and his son Telemachus during the Trojan War. When years pass and Telemachus sets out to search for his missing father, the goddess Athena assumes the form of Mentor to accompany him. The human being welcomes a human form for counsel. From its very origins, becoming a mentor is a transcendent act; it carries with it something of the holy.

The Barbera Foundation's Mentoris Project sets out on an Athena-like mission: We hope the books that form this series will be an inspiration to all those who are seekers, to those of the twenty-first century who are on their own odysseys, trying to find enduring principles that will guide them to a spiritual home. The stories that comprise the series are all deeply human. These books dramatize the lives of great Italians and Italian-Americans whose stories bridge the ancient and the modern, taking many forms, just as Athena did, but always holding up a light for those living today.

Whether in novel form or traditional biography, these books plumb the individual characters of our heroes' journeys. The power of storytelling has always been to envelop the reader in a vivid and continuous dream, and to forge a link with the subject. Our goal is for that link to guide the reader home with a new inspiration.

What is a mentor? A guide, a moral compass, an inspiration. A friend who points you toward true north. We hope that the Mentoris Project will become that friend, and it will help us all transcend our daily lives with something that can only be called holy.

—Robert J. Barbera, President, Barbera Foundation
—Ken LaZebnik, Editor, The Mentoris Project

Chapter One

A CHALLENGING CHILDHOOD

The unique success story of Amadeo Pietro Giannini's progress from enlightened self-taught man to one of the most powerful and far-sighted bankers of the twentieth century runs parallel to the transformation of his home state California from a promising but peripheral state to the leading region of the western United States, providing a fertile ground for the fulfillment of the American Dream. The seeds of his vocation and mission are traceable to his challenging childhood, which molded him into a revolutionary in the banking world.

His father, Luigi Giannini, was an immigrant of humble origins from Liguria who was lured to California by the exciting prospects of the Gold Rush, deciding in 1864 to set out from his native village of Favale di Malvaro in the Val Fontanabuona, thirty miles northeast of Genoa.

People coming to the United States in search of better lives often banded together with their own kind for some time before assimilating into the melting pot of American culture. Luigi was part of the first, most intense phase of migration to the West Coast, which took place during the middle of the nineteenth century and immediately after the unification of Italy in 1861.

Although Giuseppe Garibaldi, the great hero of the Italian *Risorgimento*, had succeeded in uniting the northern and southern parts of the peninsula, life in Italy continued to be very harsh. Unification in fact began with a heavy tax burden imposed by Rome, especially on farmers. As Deanna Paoli Gumina has pointed out in her book *Italians of San Francisco: 1850–1930*, the migratory wave to the western United States was very different from the one in which Italians settled on the Atlantic coast.[1] In New York, newly arrived Italians appeared to be destined, at least initially, to a condition of social inferiority whereas the "westbound" immigrants possessed unique professional skills and were relatively more affluent, which enabled them to bear the additional expense of crossing the continent and the physical hardships associated with resettlement; most of them became successful in a brief period of time in fishing, farming, and viniculture in the Sonoma and Napa Valleys.

When Luigi returned to California for the second time in 1868, he knew he was through searching for gold. He still wanted to settle in California and raise a family in that fertile land. He already had a girl in mind named Virginia De Martini but he had never met her in person. Luigi got to know her through the frequent letters she sent to her two brothers while he was working with them in the gold fields. While they read her intriguing correspondence around the campfire, Luigi felt a secret attraction and somehow knew she was the right person for him. He went back to Italy just to meet her, which turned out very successfully. He managed to convince her parents he was a worthy suitor: to impress them, he wore a double money belt with a supply of $20 gold pieces. After an intense six-week courtship, he married Virginia on August 10, 1869, shortly after her fifteenth birthday, in Chiavari, on the Ligurian coast. At the wedding she wore a white hat that he had brought her as a gift from America and it became the talk of the town, as Virginia's elder sister Teresa later recounted to A.P Giannini himself.[2]

They set off in 1869 for the United States, crossing the Atlantic on a third-class ticket. After docking in New York they were able to cross the country by train since the Transcontinental Railroad had just been completed, thus avoiding the treacherous route across the Isthmus of Panama with its jungle and suffocating heat. By the fall they were settled in San Jose, a frontier town in the Santa Clara valley, about fifty miles from San Francisco, and older than any other settlement in California. Luigi invested all his savings in renting and renovating a house, which he turned into the Swiss Hotel, a two-story building with twenty rooms, which catered to Italian day-laborers belonging to the steady European migration in search of riches. Many were attracted by the warm atmosphere created by the two Italian-American immigrants in a country where, notwithstanding the genuine opportunities for hard-working people, foreigners in general— and especially those of Chinese and Italian origin— were often disliked, mistrusted, looked upon with suspicion and hostility, and frequently faced open discrimination. They had to prove themselves in order to overcome all the prejudices against them.

It was in the Swiss Hotel that on May 6, 1870 the Gianninis' first son was born and christened Amadeo Pietro. After two years as the owner of the hotel, Luigi successfully sold it and with the proceeds bought forty acres of land in the small town of Alviso, eight miles north of San Jose. The Giannini farm prospered between 1871 and 1876 because of its excellent location and climate, which their motivation and hard work exploited to the fullest. They were learning English while acquiring their American citizenship. Across the state their fellow Italians were settling a number of farmlands and were to play a leading role in developing today's fruit, vegetable, and dairy industries, while also leaving their mark on the California food-processing industry.

Luigi and Virginia had all the elements for establishing themselves as an ever more solid family unit and as successful farmers. Their second son, Attilio, was born in July 1874, while Amadeo, still a toddler, loved playing outdoors and was always eager to help his parents with picking strawberries and fruit from the trees in that natural hothouse. He soon enrolled in the elementary school and enjoyed studying with children of many nationalities (Portuguese, Italian, French, German, Spanish, Armenian, Japanese, and American) who were sometimes unable to pronounce his Italian name. He had a good time, learning quickly from books and making lifelong friends. This was the environment that saw Luigi become an independent, successful farmer bringing his wagons filled with produce to Alviso, which rapidly turned from a small, sleepy town into a hub for the nationwide distribution of local produce. By 1875, the Pacific Fruit Express would carry the fruit and vegetables of the Santa Clara Valley in refrigerated carriages to the rest of the nation. Luigi became a prominent figure among the thousands of transplanted farmers who swarmed into San Jose in the decades after the Gold Rush, and was able to provide a comfortable life for his wife and children. He was proud to follow in the footsteps of his father Carlo, his grandfather Stefano, and his great-grandfather Giuseppe, who for generations had farmed the land back in their native Favale.

Luigi was a man of few words and was notably circumspect because he was aware that he was living in a racially biased environment. His life was full of promise until one afternoon in August 1876, when tragedy struck, as reported in detail by *San*

Jose Mercury and Herald, the town's leading daily.[3] His personal American dream came abruptly to an end. He was shot over a difference of one dollar in the wages of a field worker who had been hired to assist Luigi with the fruit-picking. The dispute spiraled out of control: he was confronted and gunned down in front of his own home, as Amadeo looked on with incredulous dismay. He died almost instantly, but was able to regain consciousness for a few moments and tell the police the name of the assailant, who was soon arrested and sent to jail for the rest of his life.

What kind of impact can this sudden lethal event have had in that fateful year of 1876 on Amadeo who witnessed everything unfold in front of his eyes? No biography has yet explored this key psychological turning point in full. The instant transformation of Amadeo from a carefree and innocent child into a premature adult through the painful experience of loss made him aware of his new responsibility and role in the family. From that moment, his mother, a pregnant widow of only twenty-two, bravely took over the management of the family farm while raising her small children. Amadeo was only seven at the time, Attilio was three, and George was born shortly after. Amadeo was a very sensitive boy; of the two siblings, he was the one who suffered the most: he cried himself to sleep every night. He was very grateful to be alive having unwillingly discovered how fragile human existence was, a truth that he remembered forever. The resourceful young widow was very good-looking and ambitious for herself and her children. She had already shown how brave and adventurous she was by leaving her family and homeland with a man she had known only for six weeks. The untimely death of her husband inspired her to become an excellent and self-sufficient farmer as well as a smart businesswoman; under her exceptional care the farm continued to prosper.

Amadeo wanted to be helpful at all costs and often accompanied her before dawn on the steamer going to San Francisco in the cold darkness of the Bay, to sell their fruit and vegetables. The emerging coastal trade in farm commodities at that time was a dangerous adventure necessitating a precarious sea journey along the rocky peninsula coast.[4]

Even at a tender age, Amadeo was attracted by the hubbub of the Alviso landing and even more so by the hustle and bustle of trade on the San Francisco waterfront. During the trips to the Bay Area with his mother, he seemed instinctively to prefer the energy of human interaction and commerce to the restricted life of his one-room school in Alviso.

Chapter Two

LORENZO SCATENA:
A NEW ROLE MODEL AT THE WATERFRONT

After over four years of mourning and hardship, in the summer of 1880 the family's prospects changed for the better. Virginia agreed to marry Lorenzo Scatena, a thirty-year-old Italian immigrant, originally from Lucca, who had come to San Jose at the age of twelve and worked as a hauler for a commission firm on the San Francisco waterfront. The two met while she was selling her produce and they became good friends. He was a gentle, amiable man with a ready smile and her children seemed to love and respect him to the point of calling him "Pop" or "Boss." In his turn, Lorenzo called Amadeo by his initials A.P., a nickname that stuck with him for the rest of his life. Lorenzo moved to the Giannini farm and took over some of the heaviest tasks while keeping his job as a hauler.

He formally adopted Virginia's three children and provided them with a positive father figure. He was an honest worker and made a modest living. The family soon grew from five to seven, with the birth of the first two Scatena children, Henry and Florence. After a devastating drought, the additional financial strain and the unsettled economic conditions near the end of the so-called "terrible seventies," Lorenzo decided to leave the Alviso farm and move back for a while to San Jose and try his hand at the burgeoning commission business. Virginia's frequent trips to San Francisco soon convinced her too that the city offered more opportunities for her growing family. At that time, San Francisco was one of the richest cities per capita in the world and its inhabitants could afford to pay very high prices for produce.

She was particularly fascinated by the commission merchants and their wholesale firms operating as hard-bargaining middlemen in California's fast-developing production of agricultural commodities. Their activity consisted in buying the produce at the lowest possible price from the farmers before shipping their goods to San Francisco and reselling them to grocers, street markets, and restaurants for a profit. It was a tough business but much more financially rewarding than farming.

Lorenzo and Virginia decided to sell the farm and in 1882 moved to a rented house in San Francisco on Jackson Street close to the wharfs in an effort to expand the produce business. Virginia convinced her husband to accept a job as a commission clerk with A. Galli & Sons, one of the best-established commission firms on the waterfront. He worked sixteen hours a day, from midnight until the following afternoon. It was essential for him to show up on the docks early, no later than 12:30 a.m. to buy and sell, not leaving until there was no perishable produce left to buy or sell. Scatena brought considerable natural skills to his job as wholesale trader. In recognition of his talent his monthly salary was raised from $100 to $250 a month. Virginia thought this was not enough for his exhausting nighttime work and dedication; she urged him to ask for a further raise, which was denied. She convinced him then to quit and start his own produce company. About four blocks from the waterfront he opened a few weeks later the firm L. Scatena & Co. and by the end of the first month of independent business her husband had earned $1,500, proving the far-sighted Virginia correct.

They soon moved to North Beach, an Italian neighborhood, where one of the largest Italian communities in the nation had settled, and specifically into 411 Green Street, a two-story shingled house with a large bay window, a symbol of prosperity at that time. The majority of the community was from Northern Italy—Tuscany, Piedmont, and Liguria—but a large section came also from the South, in particular from Sicily. In the beginning they worked as fishermen, shopkeepers, stonemasons, and produce sellers or commission dealers like Scatena, who in less than a year would become one of the most successful young men in the produce business.

North Beach looked like a Mediterranean seaside village next to Telegraph Hill with its steep and narrow cobblestone streets. Virginia Scatena's dream was that Lorenzo should succeed in business, which he did, and that the boys should receive the best possible education.

Of the three boys, Attilio was the most gifted student. Very early on he decided he wanted to study medicine. He was nicknamed "Doc" and would be known by this name for the rest of his life.

A.P. was also a very good student and a quick learner. He resumed his formal education at the Washington Street Grammar School in North Beach. He excelled right away in spelling and writing and was proud to do well. He was tenacious and independent by nature, friendly and serious, but his heart was not in the classroom. He became more and more interested in helping his stepfather in his business with a clever, original, and profitable approach.

When A.P. met Pop's accountant, Tim Delay, he set himself to learning about daily accounting and the importance of a correct balance sheet to verify the health of the day-to-day business. He would also spend his afternoons writing, on his own initiative, at his stepfather's desk, dozens of letters soliciting business by mail from farmers wanting to sell their crops on consignment, advertising honest prices and quick service; many of them wrote back accepting the deal. So Pop, to his great surprise, began receiving commissions from growers and this novelty yielded positive financial results. This was A.P.'s first major business venture, and it proved unexpectedly successful in securing new customers for the newly established firm.

Soon A.P. started sneaking out of the house and turning up late at night at the waterfront, tiptoeing back in through the rear door so as not to wake his mother.

He would arrive at the docks during the peak hours of business. By the light of smoky oil lamps, workers unloaded crates of fruit and vegetables from the ships. Produce sellers would hawk their goods in many languages, from Italian to Greek, from Armenian to Portuguese, and Pop would inspect them all and bargain for some of the best. A.P. realized that each steamer carried a list of its cargo and passengers; he ingeniously devised an efficient strategy to make the most out of the time spent at the wharfs. He would copy the inventory in his neat, orderly handwriting so that his father could immediately find out what produce had arrived and decide at a glance how much to buy and at what price, while his competitors were busy cursing and shouting to outbid the others with only a vague idea of what was available on a given day. He also learned the names and faces of everyone on the wharf and soaked up all the information he could get during the night. At sunrise, when the wagons carried off the produce, A.P. would rush home to have breakfast and then go to school. Virginia watched this slow but persistent drift of her son from his studies to business. She was worried he was spending too much time at the Washington Wharf and that his afternoon naps were not enough for a growing boy expected to graduate from high school.

His father came up with a challenging idea, which he was sure would definitively discourage his teenage son and put a stop to his early business aspirations. With his wife's approval he offered A.P. a gold watch if he could locate and convince any farmer who was not already a customer of the firm to sell a boxcar of oranges, considered a luxury item at the time. The best growers were located in Southern California, hundreds of miles from San Francisco. He was sure A.P. would not be able to accomplish such a difficult task, almost impossible for a fourteen-year-old boy.

A few weeks, later A.P. handed Pop not one but two consignment orders for boxcar loads of oranges from the Santa Ana Fruit Company in Tustin, Orange County. He received, as agreed, a gold watch that he cherished for the rest of his life as a memento of a successful transaction and a good omen for the future. In other words, he proved early on to have the Midas touch by literally turning oranges into gold.[5]

The pleasure and satisfaction involved in this precious reward was the driving force in his decision in the spring of 1885 to drop out of school, not to shirk educational responsibilities but simply to realize his potential. His grades at school were surprisingly good and his teachers appreciated him and put him on the honors list, often asking him to come to the blackboard to write in front of the whole class.[6]

However, his personal temperament, his ingrained love of a challenge, and his own stimulating business-oriented home environment led A.P. inevitably to an early career. Clearly he preferred to focus his intelligence and learning on practical ends. His interests in penmanship and mathematics in class found an immediate application and reward in his everyday life. "I decided school had nothing more to offer me ... I wanted to get ahead," he told an interviewer years later.[7] Despite all of Virginia's hopes for A.P. to get a college education, she had the good sense to understand the deep motivation behind her son's persistence and accept his irrevocable decision.

She did manage to convince him to enroll in a three-month course in accounting at the local Heald Business school, which was a regionally accredited business college with multiple campuses in California. The school offered courses in the fields of business, law, and technology. Eager to finish, A.P. took the final exam after only six weeks and passed it. He knew very well what he wanted to do and there was no point in putting it off.

His stepfather became his role model, his mentor, teacher, and ultimately his future business partner. The reason that A.P. abandoned his formal education at the age of fifteen was because he felt a strong entrepreneurial vocation that he needed to pursue and he had no time to waste. The waterfront of San Francisco was his school and his playground. His formative years buying and selling fruit and vegetables with his stepfather gave him a valuable experience while exposing him to the world of neglected minority workers—which would inform his entire career—and a remarkable power of negotiation and persuasion. He developed an extraordinary self-confidence and charisma, which gained him the respect and trust of farmers and wholesalers.

With regret, but also with pride, Virginia would now prepare two late dinners just before midnight for the two men of the family who now went to work. If Lorenzo Scatena had responded quickly to the commission business, his new adolescent associate did so even faster. He was gifted with rare insight, exceptional memory, and psychological and commercial intuition. He had an inborn instinct for the laws of supply and demand, a sixth sense for profit or loss in any transaction, as well as a healthy ambition.

The commission business was a demanding and tricky one. The most valuable elements of this trade were timing and the capacity for quick decisions. A.P. was very young, bursting with ideas and energy. He loved the multilingual and multicultural microcosm of the waterfront, where he would interact with a crowd of farmers and merchants, talk and listen, store and treasure all the information he could collect from men twice or three times his age, often in hard-fought arguments or fierce bidding sessions. His life consisted of arriving on the docks between eleven and midnight to make deals until early the next morning. He would also accept on behalf of L. Scatena & Co. produce on consignment or contracts for future purchases, an entirely original concept. He guaranteed that the firm would pay on time and in cash. The farmers gradually realized they could trust L. Scatena & Co. since the company honored all its promises. What was particularly unique and amazing was A.P.'s knack for remembering dates, prices, and names—not only the names of his clients, but also those of their wives and children. His aim was always to keep existing customers satisfied while at the same time trying to attract new ones. Towards the end of 1885 he became the chief salesman for L. Scatena & Co., after accompanying for a period his stepfather on purchasing trips in the

Sacramento Valley. Working in that area as a buyer for a San Francisco commission house was no easy job. During those years many leading commission merchants in this sector were hiring salespeople to solicit business in the newly settled interior areas of California. Most of the buyers A.P. was competing with were tough and experienced dealers much older than him.

A.P. passionately threw himself into this new challenge because he could foresee a host of opportunities to be grasped all around him. His father proved to be right when he sent his stepson out on his own to do a man's work. A.P. was not afraid and from the very beginning proved successful mainly because he had a unique way of doing business and was especially interested in laying a foundation of trust and good will as well as building relationships that would support his father's business over time. He was focused, determined, always on the go, either by horse, buggy, or riverboat, working more than eighteen hours a day, often skipping lunch, which he deemed a waste of valuable time.

He was always one step ahead of his competitors and able to surprise them with his intuitive deal-making. During the next two years, A.P. would broaden the range of his commercial interests to include the fertile agricultural areas of Napa and Saint Joaquin Valley, besides the Santa Clara Valley he had known so well since his childhood, down to the Los Angeles basin. No waterfront merchant had ever ventured much beyond the 200-mile radius of San Francisco to purchase produce directly from farmers but A.P. was always eager to conquer new territory.[8] He would travel from one end of California to the other with his eyes wide open, trying to learn more and more about his native land with an insatiable curiosity about the diverse crops, soil and weather conditions, and the hard-working people living there.

Both he and the state of California reflected diversity, optimism, talent, and remarkable energy.[9]

He would be away from San Francisco for weeks at a time and would visit farms that were so remote that none of his competitors would have ever considered them. He taught farmers across the state the innovative techniques for picking different crops that he had observed during his travels. He took a chance on a farmer trying to establish a grapefruit grove near Los Angeles and imported the fruit to San Francisco well before anybody knew what a grapefruit was.[10] He was able to tell a good farmer from a bad one and behave accordingly; he would develop a special feeling and understanding for farmers and their aspirations and dreams. He would buy in large quantities but, at the same time, he would not refuse to deal with odd lots of produce, usually consisting of one or two crates in a total shipment of over three hundred, which would bring some little extra money to hard-pressed farm people and their families.[11]

This understanding attitude gained him a lot of acclaim and many friends. He loved to see and taste what the earth produced in California, from the best grapes to apples and every conceivable variety of fruits and vegetable. At the same time he was a born salesman: persuasive, persistent, and always willing to go the extra mile to gain a client. This is exemplified in a famous anecdote: Once, when A.P. saw a competitor on the road heading towards a ranch, he devised a shortcut by swimming across the slough, holding his clothes above his head. By the time his competitor arrived, A.P. had already completed the papers for a successful transaction. A.P. never let anyone take a customer away from him if he could help it. Salesmanship of that sort was second nature to him.[12]

By the time he was just nineteen years old, his father offered him a one-third partnership in the firm, and at twenty-one he became full partner and was well on his way in the business world. The earnings of L. Scatena & Co. had risen exponentially after A.P. started to work full time; at the end of the first year of collaboration, net profits were $10,000; the following year they were $15,000 and two years later net profits skyrocketed to $100,000.[13] Because of A.P.'s talent and efforts in these first few years, the firm was forced to move several times into larger premises, eventually settling at 300 Washington Street, the heart of San Francisco's produce district. However, the firm's growth was not enough to satisfy him and he longed for the freedom to work independently and take bigger risks.[14] He wanted to prove his intellectual independence and vision.

In addition to his charisma, A.P. had a commanding physical presence: six feet two-and-a half inches tall, powerfully built with wavy black hair, a neatly trimmed mustache, and piercing dark eyes. He was a talented and fascinating individual who could be charming and gregarious.[15] He took pride and care in his appearance, wearing on special occasions a Prince Albert coat, a top hat and gloves, and carrying a gold-tipped cane. He had a stately presence and was certainly not unnoticed by the young women of North Beach. Although he kept a sharp eye on business, he also had keen ambitions in his private life: a successful marriage could benefit both his public and private affairs. In 1891, while attending Mass at the old Spanish church between Mason and Powell streets, A.P. spotted in the choir a pretty young lady, Clorinda Agnes Cuneo, who also happened to be the youngest daughter of Joseph Cuneo, a very wealthy Italian-American in North Beach. Joseph was an immigrant from the Genoa area, who had made a fortune in real estate.[16] A.P.

immediately "made up his mind he would never marry any other woman" and, as far as we know, she was his first and only love.[17]

Clorinda, the youngest of Joseph Cuneo's fourteen children, was a well-known singer and already engaged to a young doctor from North Beach, who at the time was in Germany doing postgraduate work. They had made plans to marry as soon he returned to San Francisco. A.P. did not consider the fiancé to be a serious problem. He initiated a relentless courtship campaign, taking Clorinda out to picnics, theatrical productions, sending flowers and candy but above all, composing ardent love letters in his impeccable handwriting. Clorinda was not initially convinced but soon became more and more attracted to his magnetic personality and self-assurance. In the end she broke off the engagement and agreed to marry A.P.

A deliberate six-month courtship to win her affection resulted in their elaborate wedding on September 12, 1892 in Old St Mary's, their parish church, consecrating a union that was to last for half a century. Later that day, after a reception at Clorinda's family home in North Beach, the newlyweds left for their two-week honeymoon by train to Carmel, an idyllic retreat along the Monterey Peninsula.[18] Once again, A.P. had overcome a challenge and defeated his competitor with the same single-minded intensity that had characterized him in business.[19]

The newlyweds moved into a small furnished house close to fashionable Russian Hill and a few months later into a more convenient Victorian-style frame house on Green Street, next to Washington Square, the heart of North Beach, a few steps away from the waterfront that continued to be the center of A.P.'s life. After one year of marriage, Clorinda gave birth to their first son, Amadeo Peter Giannini, Jr. Over the next twelve years, four more sons and three daughters, two of whom died in infancy, would complete the family.[20]

It is worth pointing out that A.P. was a one-woman man and was first attracted and inspired by Clorinda in a place of worship during a religious function. It reveals perhaps something of his deeply felt Catholic education, inherited from his parents, as well as his strong desire to start a family. The loyalty he showed throughout his life enhanced his personal integrity and a sense of responsibility not only towards his mother, stepfather, and siblings, whom he supported through university, but also towards his life-long sweetheart and their children.

Interestingly enough, A.P. had previously built his honest reputation in business since adolescence by being fair in setting prices and in dealing with people. Nobody before him—in a city that had a well-deserved reputation for corruption—had loaned money without charging any interest to farmers before their crops had been harvested. These advances were often quite high: tens of thousands of dollars were to be considered as an advance against future delivery of commodities. These loans were always granted exclusively on A.P.'s moral evaluation of the man and his professional worth as a farmer, without his realizing that he was gradually developing an original sort of proto-banking mode based on principles he never betrayed.[21] Throughout the 1890s, A.P. took advantage of California's booming economy without ever neglecting his family. He seemed to be everywhere at once, concentrating his efforts in the orange and grapefruit sectors of the south where the competition was fierce. The wholesale trade in those areas was in the hands of a few local merchants who did not have the farmers' best interests at heart. They would either refuse to honor their contracts or pay out less money than the crops were worth.

They were very resentful of A.P.'s interference and tried to discredit him as a foreigner by spreading negative rumors such as that he was a member of the Mafia or even a secret agent of the Pope, thereby fueling their anti-Catholic sentiments. He was never intimidated by their hostility and what he offered the farmers was total dependability and better prices.

His strategy had almost the precision and the discipline of a military operation. He would choose a target and elaborate a strategy to achieve his objectives. More and more farmers saw the advantages of doing business with the Scatena firm instead of the local wholesalers. A.P. gradually revealed an intense competitive streak and he managed singlehandedly to break small local monopolies with his integrity, spirit of service, and generosity. Instead of keeping farmers in the dark about prices, he would openly and honestly show them the price list for produce in San Francisco. Giannini's dedication paid off and the farmers soon came to appreciate and trust him.

New employees were hired, including former competitors who had decided to give up a highly risky, tough business to join L. Scatena & Co., which by 1899 Giannini had turned into the largest commission house in San Francisco with six-figure annual profits. Once there were no competitors left to beat in the field, he reached his goal, and his life became less interesting than in the previous decades. He was open to new ideas and began to look for new ventures. By now he was considered the waterfront's most successful commission merchant, or as he himself admitted in a later interview, "the king of the San Francisco waterfront."[22] His name had gradually become synonymous with integrity and resourcefulness.

At that time, San Francisco was reputed to be one of the most corrupt cities in the nation as a result of almost twenty years of boss rule by Blind Chris Buckley, a shrewd Irish saloon-keeper who demanded bribes and payments in exchange for not damaging properties or harming people. In the Forty-Fourth Assembly District, which included North Beach, the influence and power of Boss Buckley and his associates was felt everywhere.

A.P. firmly believed that San Francisco needed honest leaders willing to introduce reforms. He was very pleased to be recruited by James Phelan, a young, civic-minded, successful businessman who had been elected mayor of San Francisco as a reform Democrat three years earlier. Together they would defy the dominant boss in a "good government" campaign, which would seek support from businessmen and concerned citizens from all over the city. The intent was to increase the power of the mayor's office and bring back centralized authority and civic efficiency to San Francisco. Giannini joined Phelan because he saw a real opportunity to rid North Beach, by now considered a very dangerous area, of the lethal corrupting political influence of Buckley. As a rule, A.P. devoted his entire time to business, but he had come to understand that politics and business are strictly intertwined and since October and November were slow months in the commission business he accepted this diversion and challenge. He was convinced that this particular cause was in the best interests of the whole population of San Francisco. He soon proved to be a skilled and inspired civic leader. He organized a New Charter Democratic Club and for this purpose he rented the upper floor of a three-story building at the intersection of Union and Powell Street to serve as the headquarters of the North Beach "Reform Democrats." With his organizational abilities, he attracted voters to his office from all over the city.

Although he had a grasp of the big picture, he also had a fine eye for detail. Together with local leaders he worked out a strategy and arranged for rallies at shipyards and factories. Women could not vote at the time, so the campaign was focused only on men. He made it possible for candidates to meet their voters face to face to discuss important issues. Giannini pragmatically agreed to give speeches about good government in Italian and English and then interact and shake hands with the crowd. He proved able to mobilize a personal following, which deeply irritated and angered Buckley's forces, who reacted fiercely with open threats of physical violence. As a result, Giannini hired seventy-five horse-drawn wagons with his own money and recruited volunteers with rifles to escort voters to the polls and back home, to patrol the district's streets, and to guard the polling stations. Many people were unhappy and intimidated by the existing regime; they wanted a change but had been too afraid to go to the polls and vote as they wished.

After an intense, persuasive door-to-door campaign, the result of the elections was stunning. Boss Buckley's candidates were defeated and all of the Democratic Party's "good government" delegates were elected with a majority of six to one.[23] Phelan was triumphantly re-elected mayor and A.P. would mingle with the working people and shopkeepers to thank them personally with candy and cigars for their votes. As a result of this decisive campaign A.P. stepped out of relative anonymity and became well known to everyone in North Beach.

After this foray into politics, A.P. decided late in 1900 to take an early retirement, shocking all his friends. He never fully articulated the reasons for his decision.

He was financially secure because he had invested extensively in real estate and his fortune amounted to about $300,000 plus an annual income. He had also received $100,000 from the sale of his half-share in the business, with his father's approval. The purchasers were some employees who had bought in as he had himself done. He calculated that the money that would come in from rental property he owned was about $250 a month, besides which he had the regular income from the sale of his share of L. Scatena & Co. This was enough for himself and his family and he had no desire for unnecessary wealth. Throughout his career he considered money not as an end in itself but as a way to accomplish something meaningful. Money was simply a tool with which a man could build an idea into a reality.

He was convinced of a very profound truth: "I don't want to be rich. No man actually owns a fortune; it owns him." He wanted time to think, to be with his family and look for new ways of investing his talents and energies. He was thirty-one years old at the time. He had achieved the highest excellence in his field and there was no room for him to grow. He needed to reinvent himself.

Chapter Three

THE FOUNDING OF THE BANK OF ITALY

Giannini's retirement did not last long. His mind was restless and full of new ideas. He decided to explore the potentially lucrative world of San Francisco real estate, a field he had already taken an interest in during his years in the commission trade. He rented a desk at the city's oldest and most respected real estate firm, Madison and Burke, to learn more about this possible career path. Eventually he opened a small office of his own and persuaded his stepfather to be part of this enterprise, buying and selling houses to friends, old business associates, and others throughout the city who knew his reputation for reliability. All the elements were in place for him to become a real estate tycoon, but fate had other plans. In 1902, a new field of activity opened for energies too robust for retirement, following the death of Giannini's father-in-law, Joseph Cuneo, who left behind a real estate empire, a personal wealth of over $1 million, a widow, eleven children, and no will. This sad and sudden event would profoundly change the trajectory of Giannini's life.

A.P. was made executor of Cuneo's assets as his father-in-law, who had a profound respect for Giannini, would have wished, and the entirety of the wealth was kept intact for ten years. The agreement seemed peculiar as Cuneo had adult sons with successful businesses, but his widow was convinced that A.P. could further increase the value of the assets, including a hundred separate properties, because of his proven business acumen. The task was not easy.

In addition to real estate, Cuneo's holdings included a large block of shares and directorship in a small local bank in North Beach called Columbus Savings and Loan. Giannini decided to accept, thinking that the position would allow him to hold a prestigious title while at the same time helping society.

San Francisco at the turn of the century was the money capital of the west because of its booming industries, and therefore offered unlimited possibilities for expansion. Initially, A.P. was welcomed with open arms by the other directors of the bank because of his commercial experience and high standing among Italian-Americans in the neighborhood. At his insistence, his stepfather, Lorenzo Scatena, at that time one of the most successful businessmen in town, was also appointed to the board.

The bank catered almost exclusively to the Italian community and was the first to be established in North Beach, founded in 1893 by John Fugazi, one of the best-known Italian-Americans in the West. Fugazi settled in North Beach in the 1850s and became very successful by opening his own travel agency, the Agenzia Fugazi, which soon expanded its operations across the country. Fugazi owned one of the very few iron safes in the community and therefore became a "banker" to North Beach clients who wanted to store their precious assets for safekeeping and send money to relatives in Italy. It was a natural transition then to open Columbus Savings and Loan, serving the specific needs of his community. The Columbus Savings and Loan was rigidly conservative with extremely restrictive lending practices and was obviously more inclined to make large loans to favored prosperous clients rather than small loans to average Italian residents.

In 1899, a second Italian bank was opened by Alfred Sbarboro to further meet the needs of the community by providing small mortgages. This modest undertaking was an important step away from Fugazi's traditional and exclusive banking model. The humbler citizens, no matter how deserving, had up to then only one additional option for loans: being driven into the arms of loan sharks and usurers who charged exorbitant interest rates. At the age of thirty-two A.P. took over his father-in-law's position as a director and shareholder of the Columbus Savings and Loan Society. He knew nothing about banking but immediately realized its services had little to do with the ordinary citizens of the area. It was well known that all the big San Francisco banks, both American such as Crocker-Woolworth, Wells-Fargo, and Nevada National, and European banks like Rothschilds of London and Lazard Frères of Paris, were only for the very wealthy since they were pouring huge sums of money into mining, real estate, and costly public works projects.

The Columbus Savings and Loans Society was no exception. It was mainly a depository of valuables and paid very little interest on deposits. If a loan was ever granted high rates would be charged. For the next two years, A.P. suggested that a wide range of changes be made to its policies, but soon began expressing his dissatisfaction with how the bank was run. He wanted the bank to pursue a bold new strategy of deposit and lending that would maintain close ties with the community. Most of the Italian-Americans of North Beach were still poor and uneducated but very thrifty and hardworking. Giannini was convinced that it was essential to win the friendship and support of the common people and persuade them that they needed to rely on a trustworthy bank rather than hiding their money under their mattresses or in their teapots. Most North Beach residents had to do without the services of a bank since small loans were considered a mere nuisance and not worth the time or the profit.

A.P. felt strongly that Columbus Savings and Loan Society was operating far below its earning potential and passionately tried to influence the management to take advantage of the social and economic changes rapidly transforming North Beach, which offered limitless economic expansion.

He directly contacted new customers, particularly of the lower middle class, who truly needed the money and had never set foot in a bank before. He was convinced that more money should be lent to deserving customers and that standard minimum rates should be charged. In the long run, both the customers and the bank would prosper in all possible ways.

The disagreement between Giannini and the board gradually escalated. Part of the trouble was the fact that the chairman Isaias Hellman also managed the Nevada Bank on a similarly outdated business model, so when A.P. approached him privately his radical ideas were flatly rejected. He was accused of being an overly critical, ambitious outsider, and an arrogant troublemaker. Had the bank not managed well enough before his appointment to the board? By the spring of 1904, in spite of the fact that several of the directors, including his father, supported his plans, and more and more people of his choosing were included in the board, the friction became unbearable. Calling a surprise board meeting with most of A.P.'s friends absent, the opposition decided to oust his absent father from the director's chair thinking this would bring A.P. to heel. At this critical moment Giannini had discovered that one of the directors of the bank was making money on the side by taking commissions on loans that he himself had recommended, and he saw with his own eyes other clear examples of intolerably unethical behavior.

Giannini resigned and the board was happy to see him go. "I might never have gone into the banking business if I hadn't gotten so mad at those directors," he later recalled. This decision catapulted him out of his brief retirement and had extraordinary consequences. Giannini stormed out of his last Columbus directors' meeting, disgusted with their short-sightedness and selfish behavior and he went straight to the office of James J. Fagan. Fagan was the well-regarded Irish vice president of the American National Bank, one of the largest financial institutions, who had administered his own private account as well as that of the Scatena firm. Their friendship dated back to A.P's earliest years on the waterfront. Giannini, in spite of being a complete outsider in the financial milieu, said impetuously: "Giacomo, I'm going to start a bank. Tell me how to do it."[24] Fagan objected by pointing out that there were already too many banks in San Francisco but Giannini knew from that very moment that his bank would be different from any other, a bank for people who had never used one. This way he would fulfill his dream by servicing other hard-working, discriminated-against immigrants and turn them into a new affluent working class, which would fuel California's growth.

To set up a bank in the early 1900s was considerably simpler than it is now. Fagan helped to fill out the legal paperwork and complete the formalities for the necessary incorporation of his new savings and commercial bank, while Giannini raised $150,000 from his stepfather and ten friends as part of the initial operating capital of $300,000; the latter was divided into three thousand shares at $100 each. A board of eleven directors made up of local Italian businessmen, including five former directors from Columbus Savings and Loan, as well as James Fagan, the only non-Italian, was assembled. They all welcomed the passionate Giannini's plan without any reservations, and put their money, time, and moral backing behind him. His father assured A.P of his support on one condition: "When a poor man enters your bank he must always receive the same courtesy and consideration a rich man would get ... I want your word on it." On the basis of this profoundly ethical request, A.P. exacted from his associates a pledge: "This bank must and will be run solely for the benefit of its stockholders and depositors." What is more, "No man will be permitted to win power enough to dominate its policies unwisely. No officer, including myself, shall be tied up with outside interests. We will attend only to the business of banking. We will be servants of the depositors and stockholders and all profits will go to them."

Since North Beach already had two Italian banks, Giannini needed all the help he could get. Over the next few weeks he hired James Cavagnaro as the newly founded bank's lawyer, and in addition to his stepfather, a number of people close to him such as Charles Grondona, a local realtor, and George Caglieri, an accountant. Throughout the summer of 1904, Giannini would meet his partners at different locations to prevent Fugazi from sabotaging his plans. Once all the details were sorted out, he defiantly settled on a North Beach saloon for its strategic location at the intersection of Washington Street and Columbus Avenue, inside the Drexler building that also housed Fugazi's Columbus Savings and Loans. The newly founded bank was about one block from the city jail, and therefore also profited from the police patrolling the area night and day, offering excellent protection at no additional cost.

After first wanting to name his infant bank *Italian Bank of California*, he decided for a stronger identification with the

North Beach community and registered it as *Bank of Italy*. Soon after, Giannini persuaded the owner of the Drexler to lease him the entire building. One morning Fugazi arrived at his bank to discover to his dismay that he had become the tenant of one of his former directors and that Giannini had tripled the rent on his lease. He had no choice but to move out of the building and leave the Bank of Italy triumphant at one of the busiest intersections in town. Adding insult to injury, Giannini hired the former assistant cashier of the Fugazi bank, Armando Pedrini, as chief cashier. Pedrini accepted the job after Giannini doubled his salary and agreed to pay the difference out of his own pocket until Pedrini had proved his worth to the bank.[25] Pedrini was intelligent and qualified and had learned his professional skills in Italy and South America; he knew several languages and understood what it was like to be a stranger in a new country. A.P. above all saw in Pedrini an example of Italian politeness and charm, and his ability to give as much attention to a man in overalls as to a businessman in a suit. Giannini wanted to turn the bank's previously frigid "undertaker's parlor" atmosphere of which he was so critical into a warm, welcoming, friendly environment, and he was ready to pay the price.

His bank was remodeled into an efficient medium-sized room with no private enclosed offices, and included just three desks, a few chairs, and a single teller's window. This essential layout had been designed on an open plan so as not to intimidate the customers and to enable him to meet the needs of ordinary people, rather than the local elite and, indirectly, the institutions of Wall Street. His customers were neither wealthy nor powerful. A.P., being himself the son of hard-working Italian farmers, founded his own bank mainly because he was outraged by how other banks in North Beach neglected the Italian citizens of San Francisco's Italian colony, which included his own family. The majority of his customers were immigrants who could hardly speak English, elsewhere despised and distrusted, and who were intimidated by the banking system. He did not go into this new business venture to make money for himself but to serve his community.[26] A motto he had loved since he was a teenager was: "Serving the needs of others is the only legitimate business today." No loan was too small and no customer was too poor to receive careful consideration. The humble were entitled to the same attention as the rich. This radically innovative attitude turned him into the inventor of microcredit, which proved beneficial to the individual and the collective alike.

Giannini at that time was worth between $200,000 and $300,000. The house—later called Seven Oaks by Clorinda—that he purchased for $20,000 in suburban San Mateo, where he lived with his family, was spacious and comfortable but not ostentatious. That was all the money and property Giannini intended ever to have. When he died in 1949, at the age of 79, he still lived in the same house and left an estate of about $490,000, meaning he was worth less than when he opened the Bank of Italy, if the depreciation of the dollar is taken into account.

He ruled the bank not by force of money but by his egalitarian democratic vision and philosophy. His bank was his extended family and his employees were his "boys and girls." They were all motivated by the same goal of serving and educating the community.

Giannini was uniquely responsible for realizing a social utopia, which in time radically changed the lives of millions of people who learned how to overcome poverty by working and saving, and by borrowing money to venture into pioneering new projects, hitherto considered beyond their reach.

A.P.'s imagination transcended that of most bankers of his day because it evolved daily and branched out into a number of extraordinary innovations for customers, some of whom were so involved in the life of the bank that they became stockholders and therefore co-owners of a financial institution.

When at 9 a.m. on Monday, October 17, 1904, the newly founded institution that he proudly called *Bank of Italy* opened its doors to the public, the salaried employees were only three. Giannini, as vice president and manager, received no salary, nor did any of the other directors on the board. The new bank catered right away to grocers, bakers, stonemasons, shoemakers, plumbers, barbers, and fishermen as well as dock workers, some of whom were almost illiterate, at least in their adopted language.

The employees patiently taught customers how to fill out deposit slips and other forms, after explaining that it was more profitable to deposit their savings at the bank rather than to hide their extra coins at home in jars or cans because the bank paid interest. A small amount of labor-free extra cash every month is a pleasant bonus for people used to working extremely hard to make their money. The Bank of Italy was willing to make loans as small as twenty-five dollars and accept deposits of any amount; the customers were encouraged to do so knowing that they could withdraw their money in case of need. They came to believe in Giannini and were won over by his trust-based approach to banking. He was convinced that working class citizens, though lacking in assets against which to guarantee loans, were generally honest and would pay back their loans when they could. Further, by granting loans, he helped his clients to better themselves in ways they would not have been able to do without that money, such as buying a home or starting a business.

He was always the first to arrive in the morning and the last to leave the premises at night. He spoke their language. He would walk the streets of San Francisco along with Charley Grondona, the Bank's secretary, encouraging people to deposit their savings in his bank because they could earn money simply by opening an account there. Many recognized him from his days on the wharfs or the Boss Buckley campaign. They would listen to him because of his knowledge, common sense, and courtesy. Banks at that time did not solicit accounts. They would never stoop to the level of advertising themselves but Giannini took the opposite approach.

He was eager to inform people by word of mouth, newspaper or any other medium and explain in English or Italian the functions and unprecedented services of his new bank. He used to say "How can people know what a bank can and will do for them unless they're told?" At the end of the first day of business, Bank of Italy had accepted deposits of $8,780 mainly from a local group of fish merchants as well as from his mother, his sister-in-law, and employees. Soon after, thousands of dollars began to emerge from hiding places, drawing a steady 3.5% interest for their owners, to be in turn lent by the bank to others. As the bank's reputation for fair dealing spread, large accounts were also opened. On the whole, the deposits were the kind Giannini had hoped for: the small savings of many small people or as Giannini himself used to say, of "the little fellow." By the end of 1905, the resources of the bank amounted to $1,000,000, of which more than $700,000 were in commercial accounts and savings.[27]

Things were going so well that Giannini raised the salaries of all the employees, now six in number, and Pedrini's full salary was paid directly by the board of directors. He wanted to give a chance not only to the Italian Americans to gradually integrate into the mainstream but also to all the other ethnic groups in San Francisco. Thus, he used to say: "We're here to do business with everybody and anybody who needs our help—regardless of nationality or place of business or newness or smallness."

North Beach was growing at the rate of two thousand people every year and A.P. saw these newcomers as potential customers because they needed help settling in a new country. Most of them were poor and spoke no English when they arrived, but were determined to make a better life for themselves. He knew from his own family's example that in a few years most of these immigrants would prosper and become grateful clients of the institution that had given them a start. This was the right time to win their loyalty, when the big banks of the area would look down on them with suspicion and disdain. His vision was also closely tied to his expectations about California's future, which in his mind included the promise of an almost limitless economic expansion.

He felt that most other banks did not grasp that a huge untapped mass market was growing in the West. The Gold Rush had generated hundreds of millions of dollars in ore, the state was also by now an agricultural powerhouse, an important trader with the Far East, and a good place to do business. He recognized that in the twentieth century, large profits could be made by catering to millions of people with modest means. His perception was crystal clear and free of doubt to the point that he was truly ready for a sort of a moral bet on the future of his compatriots. As Gerald Nash acutely points out: "In his recognition of the potentials of a mass market rather than those of a class market, he was at least a generation ahead of most others."[28] His clairvoyance, a rare gift, along with his psychological insight, entrepreneurial ability, resilience, and managerial skills constituted the formula for his growing personal and financial success.

The decision to devote his talents and inexhaustible energy to banking was very significant not only for himself, but in time also for California, the West, and the whole American banking system. Almost everything he had done so far was a very fruitful preparation for this new challenging career. In retrospect, his hard bargaining as a commission merchant, his expertise in real estate, and his involvement, though brief, in local politics had added much to his multifaceted talents. At the Columbus Savings and Loan Society he learnt the hard way how *not* to run a bank in the new century and his insatiable curiosity and profound desire to elevate his own community launched him into a career that was much broader in scope than the limiting fruit commission business he had retired from. With his wide-ranging contacts he was able to recruit scores of new customers, just as he had in his resourceful adolescence. What really alerted the San Francisco banking fraternity was a fast-moving phenomenon. The depositors of the North Beach area flocked to the new bank from its first month of opening.

Undoubtedly A.P.'s success was largely due to his magnetic personality and generosity. He genuinely hoped to improve the lives of thousands of individuals, including the children of immigrants like himself. However, he was fortunate enough to operate in a robust economic environment that favored entrepreneurial experimentation. The first decade of the century marked another era of prosperity for much of California and the West, after the severe depression of the 1890s. One million newcomers settled on the East Coast, mainly in New York and Boston, while the population of the seventeen states west of the Mississippi River grew from 6.3 million in 1900 to 17.9 million twenty years later.[29] This was a time for change, for action, and therefore the fortuitous entry of Giannini into the financial world also came at the perfect juncture from a historical point of view. His restless drive to serve and educate his clients as well as to make a profit for the bank and its customers, combined with a human touch, had a distinctive appeal. The prospect of developing a satisfied and well-informed network that looked to him for a variety of essential services had become a reality, and throughout 1904 and 1905 the bank enjoyed a slow but steady growth.

Giannini devoted the bulk of the Bank of Italy's capital to individual real estate loans, also granting a number of unsecured personal loans that he called "character loans" to borrowers he instinctively trusted. Only a year and a half after the newly founded bank opened its doors, loans exceeded deposits by more than $200,000. He was particularly pleased as well with the bank's wide distribution of stocks and in particular with those small investors who bought just a few shares each. He was aiming at broadly based ownership, therefore if someone, especially North Beach Italians, felt left out, he would persuade some of his directors to surrender part of their own shares to fulfill his policy of wide distribution, establishing in this way a revolutionary new democracy in banking. No one from within the bank was allowed to borrow one cent of the bank's money. He did not want any speculative sprees with the funds of his institution. For a time A.P. and his father worked without salary and the bank prospered.

Ultimately 1906 proved so lucrative that the board of directors granted Giannini a salary of $200 a month, even though he dedicated all his time to work and continued on a daily basis to put in his own money, which would only be refunded fifteen years later.

Chapter Four

THE EARTHQUAKE: DISASTER AND OPPORTUNITY

April 21, 1906, was the day on which two thousand paid-up shares were scheduled to be distributed, but a major and unforeseen event took place, upsetting everyone's plans.[30] At 5:18 a.m. on April 18, 1906, the people of the Bay Area were literally tossed out of bed amid the chaos of an unprecedented earthquake that on today's Richter scale would correspond to a magnitude spanning from 7.8 to as high as 8.3. Even though the first jolt lasted only twenty-eight seconds, these seemed an eternity and the lethal consequences of San Francisco's greatest natural disaster would resonate for years.

San Francisco, unanimously recognized as queen of the Golden West, had been at that time the ninth-largest city in the United States and the largest on the West Coast. Over a period of sixty years, the city had become the financial, trade, and cultural center of the west as well as the "gateway to the Pacific," with the busiest port on the West Coast through which growing U.S. economic and military power was projected into the Pacific and Asia.

Windows shattered and fell out. Sidewalks buckled and the streets were cluttered with tangled wires as well as uprooted telephone and power poles. The flimsy structures from the time of the Gold Rush, hastily built by the Forty-Niners, collapsed immediately. The same happened to the houses south of Market Street that were built on reclaimed land, former bay marshes, which had been packed with soil to gain more ground. These homes slipped from their foundations and in no time were reduced to splintered boards, from which burst the initial flames of another immediate assault, an uncontrollable fire. North of Market Street the shoddy tenement houses and shacks of the twenty thousand Chinese immigrants who were crammed into a few blocks burned quickly as the fire relentlessly consumed what the earthquake had left behind.

Many water pipes had cracked and split. Under these circumstances, the San Francisco firefighters had a near-impossible task. Much of their equipment was unusable because it was buried beneath mountains of rubble. They were also left leaderless as Dennis Sullivan, the Fire Chief, running to check on his wife as the earthquake struck, was caught up in it himself and died later in the hospital. Since San Francisco had already experienced six major devastating fires, Chief Sullivan had long been concerned about the city's water supply. He had battled for years to get a supplementary salt-water system, but he was all but ignored by the local political authorities. In fact, the availability of water that day was limited to very few working hydrants and was nowhere near sufficient; hoses were instantly rigged to draw water from the San Francisco Bay, which saved most of the waterfront but was not much help further inland.[31]

Consequently, the mayor of San Francisco, Eugene E. Schmitz, the first Union Labor mayor in U.S. history, begged for urgent help from the naval station on the nearby Mare Island, letting everybody know that in San Francisco there was no water, no communication infrastructure, and that the entire phone system was compromised. He also sent urgent telegrams to the mayor of Oakland, Frank Mott, asking for fire engines and dynamite, announcing that the whole city was doomed and that Golden Gate Park was already one vast hospital. At the time, only 375 deaths were reported, partly because hundreds of fatalities in Chinatown went unrecorded. The total number of deaths is still uncertain today, and is estimated to be 3,000 at the minimum. Most of the deaths occurred in San Francisco itself, but almost 200 were reported elsewhere in the Bay Area.

In the midst of this inferno, Mayor Schmitz promptly ordered that five thousand copies of a very important proclamation be widely distributed that very day, requesting all citizens to remain at home from darkness until daylight for safety reasons. He also instructed the Gas and Electric Lighting Companies not to turn on any gas or electricity. He warned the citizens of the danger of fire and requested the Chief of Police, Jeremiah Dinan, to shoot looters at sight. Crowds of frightened citizens gathered in the streets. People streamed down Market Street, hoping to catch the ferry crossing the bay to Oakland. Among them was the great tenor Enrico Caruso, who was tossed from his bed in the old Palace Hotel. When he met Armando Pedrini and Ettore Avenali, on their way to work at the Bank of Italy, he had recovered enough to appreciate their joke that he himself had set off the quake with his powerful voice the night before.[32]

Caruso was in San Francisco along with the entire traveling company of New York's Metropolitan Opera, which lost all of its costumes and sets. The previous evening Caruso—already a worldwide sensation—had sung the part of Don José in Bizet's *Carmen* at the Mission Opera House. He went to bed that night feeling pleased about his performance and looking with pride at the photograph President Theodore Roosevelt had dedicated to him. "But what an awakening!" he wrote in the account published later that spring in London's *The Sketch*. "I wake up about 5 o'clock, feeling my bed rocking as though I am in a ship on the ocean ... I get up and go to the window, raise the shade and look out. And what I see makes me tremble with fear. I see the buildings toppling over, big pieces of masonry falling, and from the street below I hear the cries and screams of men and women and children." He vowed to never return to San Francisco after this nightmare.

The tremors were also felt, albeit slightly less intensely, in San Mateo, seventeen miles from the epicenter of San Francisco. Giannini was thrown out of bed at dawn as the house at Seven Oaks was shaken to its foundations. The chimney had collapsed, along with parts of the roof. Clorinda was expecting her eighth child and A.P., with reassuring words, hushed their two sons Mario and Virgil and the latest addition, Claire, who were scared to death. Luckily the rest of the house had not been seriously damaged. He made sure that Clorinda and the children would be safe with the neighbors while he planned to try to reach the city. The train crawled along for a few miles at a snail's pace before coming to a halt at the old station at Twenty-Second and Valencia Street, several miles from North Beach. A.P. had no choice but to proceed on foot; a journey that usually lasted thirty minutes took him five hours. He arrived at the bank exactly at noon, fighting his way, step by step, through a panicked crowd.

Armando Pedrini and Ettore Avenali had hurried to the Bank as soon as they woke up, and they were amazed to find the building still intact. They tried to guess what Giannini would have done if he had been present. They decided that the earthquake should not stop the Bank of Italy from opening. So they followed their daily routine of stopping at Crocker-Woolworth National, San Francisco's largest bank where some $300,000 of the Bank of Italy funds were kept in the vaults. The old iron safes of the Bank of Italy looked secure to customers but they were truly not much more than "cracker boxes without tops," to quote Giannini's own words.[33] Leaving the money every night at Crocker-Woolworth had been decided as a necessary protection measure. That morning they retrieved from the vaults not only the necessary cash to do business but all the assets of the Bank of Italy including gold and silver in three heavy pouches, amounting to approximately $80,000. Not without difficulties, they brought the whole treasure back safely to their premises at Columbus and Washington, in the usual buggy pulled by a white mare named Dolly Gray, which was considered part of the family and belonged to Clarence Cuneo, Clorinda's brother.[34] Thousands of people were trying to flee to safety. They loaded their possessions into trunks and suitcases and pulled them noisily over the uneven cobblestones. That morning there were no cable cars; the tracks running down San Francisco's main thoroughfares were twisted and warped and no trolleys could pass.

At 9 a.m., Pedrini and Avenali opened the doors and were ready to get to work but they soon realized that a number of fires had started in the city and people were rushing frantically back and forth trying to move their personal belongings to safety, inevitably clogging the streets. They noticed smoke rising from south of Market but were alarmed only later when the smell of smoke became stronger. Business was slow, but the bank remained open. As soon as he reached the bank three hours later, Giannini breathed a sigh of relief when he saw that the bank had only minor damage but he was concerned by his employees' independent decision to remove the bank's assets from Crocker-Woolworth, which he considered more secure. Looters had already started prowling and the soldiers had not yet moved in from the fort. He left Pedrini inside on guard with closed doors and a trusty six-shooter for protection while he went out with Avenali in search of news.

He wanted to check how far the fires might spread. The Fire Department had already rushed into several buildings in nearby areas and ordered everyone out. Explosions rumbled. Dense clouds of smoke rose in the distance. The flames had already reached Clay and Sansome and there was a brisk wind blowing. Nothing, except dynamite and artillery, could fight the fire, which was starting to eat up large sections of the city, burning alive those who were still trapped in the rubble. The Niantic building was already a tall torch of flames. He knew he had to move quickly. His practical mind figured out right away that "they had about two hours to get out of there," as he recalled later, and decided that the best thing was to try to transport all the bank's assets to his own home in San Mateo.

Some of the fires that morning had been provoked by the turmoil of the seismic shaking and by broken electric wires, others by the dynamite used by the firemen who had felt helpless without water and tried in some way to stop the blaze. Others were started deliberately by the inhabitants of San Francisco once they realized their homes had been destroyed. At that time, damage from earthquakes was excluded from coverage under most insurance policies; only fire damage was refundable. Insurance companies, faced with staggering claims of $250 million, eventually paid out between $235 million and $265 million on policyholders' claims, mostly for fire damage only. At least 137 insurance companies were directly involved, 20 of which went bankrupt. The fire following the earthquake in San Francisco cost altogether an estimated $350 million at the time, equivalent to almost $9 billion today.

Giannini was convinced there was not one secure spot left in San Francisco. He contacted Scatena and asked for two teams of horses, two wagons, and several crates of fruit and vegetables. At nearly five in the afternoon the two wagons were waiting in front of the bank and A.P. and his staff loaded the bank's cash, gold and silver, records, books, and stationery at the bottom as well as one typewriter, one adding machine, and light fixtures and then placed the produce crates on top.

There was no use looking back. Since chaos was spreading in the city, A.P. decided to wait until dark before trying to reach San Mateo, and A.P. and Pedrini steered one of the vehicles while Cuneo and A.P.'s brother George directed the other through side streets and detours towards the apartment of Clarence Cuneo, his brother-in-law, at Francisco and Jones Streets. That section had so far been spared by the fires. Mrs. Cuneo gave them a quick supper and then they loaded more furnishings and mattresses to give the appearance of a refugee caravan. By 8 p.m., they were on their way out of San Francisco. The two teams struggled, dragging their heavy loads along the Presidio, a much longer route, trying to avoid the debris and masses of panic-stricken people. The trip, which would normally take three hours by wagon, lasted the entire night. To the utterly exhausted men, it seemed that the world was ending.

At 7 a.m. the next day, they plodded through the gateway of Seven Oaks. A.P. had successfully managed to bring his bank home on wheels but there was no safe in the house so he stashed the cash and the three canvas bags containing gold and silver in the ash pit of the fireplace in the living room. The men stood guard around the house. They hardly slept but all was quiet. He had never felt so relieved in his life. He had succeeded in rescuing all his customers' savings and he felt a profound obligation to inform them and help rebuild the city as soon as possible. Rest was not for him under such exceptionally dire circumstances. Cuneo's buggy and his favorite mare, Dolly Gray, took him back to town after he had slept for just a few hours. Fires had raged incessantly. He returned to see that the Bank of Italy, in spite of surviving the earthquake, was now a mass of charred rubble. Most of the city's banks, including Crocker-Woolworth, had burned down, along with theaters, libraries, courts, jails, schools, churches, and convents as well as 250,000 homes. All the warehouses and manufacturing plants south of Market Street had been destroyed, including L. Scatena & Co.

Over 80% of the city was destroyed by the earthquake and ensuing fire, including the new San Francisco City Hall and landmark buildings such as the famed Palace Hotel, whose sumptuous wood-paneled rooms burnt down, despite the presence of water sprinklers and large cisterns on the roof. Only very few buildings in the business district survived because they had been built with particularly solid materials and on stable foundations. Giannini's bank was the only one to survive the catastrophe with all of its assets intact.

Around 300,000 people were left homeless out of a population of about 410,000; half of those who evacuated fled across the bay to Oakland and Berkeley. On April 19, the three major San Francisco dailies moved out of necessity across the Bay to Oakland, and issued a special joint edition entitled the *Call-Chronicle-Examiner* describing Golden Gate Park, the Presidio, Fort Mason, and the beaches near North Beach as being covered with refugee tents. On its front page, a special declaration of President Roosevelt was reported: the city had been placed under martial law and federal troops had been ordered to patrol the streets of San Francisco.

On April 21, Giannini attended an emergency meeting with all the representatives of the great banks at the residence of Henry C. Scott, the director of Crocker-Woolworth in a building near the waterfront. The mood was grim because the vaults of the banks could not be opened safely for at least several weeks and it would be months before the banks were fully operational again. Governor George Pardee had declared a bank holiday in order to devise a suitable strategy for recovery and meet the customers' needs. Across San Francisco Bay, banks in Oakland had opened for business but withdrawals were limited to thirty dollars per client.

Amid such desolation, there was a general atmosphere of bewilderment and insecurity. Giannini thought that the real asset of a bank was not really just its cash holdings but the degree to which it provided its customers with a sense of security. He believed in a psychological rather than a strictly financial resolution to this issue and proposed to intervene immediately. Once again Giannini revealed his intuitive grasp of human psychology. Unlike his colleagues who agreed on the six-month moratorium, he announced that there was no time to waste in this emergency and that he fully intended to set up a desk on the Washington Street wharf by the next day, proclaiming: "Any man who wants to rebuild San Francisco can come there and get as much cash as he needed to do so. I advise all of you bankers to beg, borrow or steal a desk and follow my example." He marched out of the meeting and went to his San Mateo home to finalize his strategy. The following morning he brought $10,000 in cash from Seven Oaks to a temporary desk—two barrels with a plank of wood on top—on which he deliberately dropped a heavy bag of gold.

There on the wharfs he set up a sign announcing that the Bank of Italy was open for business again, becoming therefore the first financial institution to reopen its 'doors.' At the same time, he placed advertisements in local newspapers and sent circulars out to inform his clientele of his Washington Street Wharf Branch Desk and that their money was safe. He and the gold were a welcome and reassuring sight.[35] He would console his compatriots, greeting his customers by name, beg them not to leave but to stay, and optimistically promised, "we are going to rebuild San Francisco and it will be better than ever."[36] He helped the city rise from the ashes by making loans "on a face and a signature" to the small businesses and people whose lives were shattered. While the executives of other banks behaved like sleepwalkers in a fog, word of the open-air bank spread quickly in North Beach. Giannini himself handed out cash, not checks or drafts, to his customers and offered unsecured loans to anyone who desired to rebuild, in this way projecting confidence, strength, and a trust that was contagious. Men clustered about his desk on the pier. His gesture won him respect and admiration from many working-class families, all of which later helped him launch the biggest bank in the world.

From that moment on, his brother Attilio "Doc" who was successfully building a medical practice in San Francisco was pulled into the banking picture and agreed to put up a sign on his apartment at 2748 Van Ness Avenue as a second location for the temporary Bank of Italy, to house the books and take care of mail. A.P. also managed to draft his youngest brother George from the produce business into the fold, restructuring the Bank into a true family enterprise. He was determined to turn the Great Catastrophe into a great opportunity not only for his bank but above all for his trusting customers. Within days, the Bank of Italy was fully operational again.

While other bankers waited for insurance companies to pay their claims, he decided to use his contacts from his commission days. A.P. had the brilliant foresight to call upon several ship captains in the Bay and lend them cash to purchase lumber in Washington and Oregon at a low price before a rebuilding campaign would inevitably monopolize the market. By the time their loads arrived in the Bay Area, they would already have been sold at a good profit, which allowed them to borrow the same amount of money again from the Bank of Italy. Giannini refused to take any profit for himself. When the San Francisco rebuilding boom got underway months later, skyrocketing the price of building materials, North Beach residents had already begun the task of rebuilding their homes and businesses at much lower prices. *L'Italia*, the largest Italian daily newspaper in San Francisco, estimated that during the period from April 1906 to March 1907, some seven hundred building permits valued at approximately $4 million were granted to North Beach Italian residents.[37] Less than a year later, North Beach became the first of the city's large residential districts to rebuild itself.[38]

No advertising campaign could have accomplished what the earthquake did for Giannini and his business. Because of his immediate intervention and far-sighted strategies in the midst of disaster, Giannini was hailed as the hero of North Beach and praised as the area's "most progressive businessman" in *L'Italia*.

Within a month, A.P. was ready to undertake the physical rebuilding of his bank. In the meantime, he found a sound building just across the street from his old quarters; the structure had survived because it was near the U.S. Post Office, which the federal troops had protected. By June 1906, while many of his competitors were still struggling, A.P's institution was busy and thriving.[39] Every day he would personally authorize loans to old and new customers. Since so many had lost everything, including identification papers, Giannini gave these people loans based on nothing more than a signature and a handshake. And surprisingly enough, every single loan he made in this way was ultimately repaid in full.

More than ever, he was impressed with the courage of ordinary people in helping themselves, if given half a chance.[40] The condition was that they should raise half of the amount they needed on their own, and in this way he accomplished two goals. On one hand, he was able to grant loans and keep his customers satisfied without running out of money; on the other, he would turn his customers into active forgers of their own destiny. This approach inspired a number of refugees to become new customers—many of whom previously mistrusted formal banking—and to deposit whatever they had since they believed that their precious assets would be in danger under a tent or temporary camp.[41] Six weeks after the earthquake, people were paradoxically depositing more money than they were withdrawing. In spite of the calamity, the number of savings accounts doubled in 1906.[42]

Although San Francisco rebuilt quickly and politicians and business owners did everything to downplay the earthquake, the disaster diverted trade, industry, and population growth south to Los Angeles, which during the twentieth century became the largest and most important urban center in the West. It was the San Francisco earthquake and its dramatic impact that confirmed Giannini's decision to embark on a lifelong career as a banker because of the response of the citizens of San Francisco. The city as a whole had finally found out what a people's bank could accomplish, and resolved to back the institution that had backed them when they needed it.[43] By the end of 1906, all the other banks were back in business and doing well while the Bank of Italy doubled its business, with a staggering number of new depositors.[44] After the apocalypse, Giannini's indomitable will saw San Francisco rise again from its ashes with new vigor and strength. In this spirit, he envisioned that his own bank would be different from anything the existing financial world had ever experienced. Giannini would honestly use every single penny of the "people's money" entrusted to his care only to protect the people's interest. In order to do so, it was essential also to try to clean up the widespread political corruption. At that time the mayor of San Francisco was Eugene Schmitz, who had been elected thanks to Abraham 'Abe' Ruef, an American lawyer and politician, who gained notoriety as the political boss behind the Schmitz administration before and after the 1906 earthquake. He ruthlessly extorted protection money from saloons, gambling houses, and brothels and ruthlessly used the tools of intimidation and violence. Surprisingly enough, even public corporations ended up submitting to his blackmail and became corrupt just to keep their immunities and privileges. Giannini, along with a group of engaged citizens, was at the forefront of this civic battle. With the support of President Roosevelt, a federal investigation was started into the corruption of City Hall because by now Abe Ruef's political machine had gained control of the Chief of Police and several judges, spreading its tentacles everywhere. Ever since the Gold Rush of 1849, San Francisco had not shaken off its reputation as a frontier town.

This finally led to Schmitz's conviction and removal from the mayor's office and Ruef's prosecution and imprisonment for bribery in 1907. After beating Boss Buckley back in 1899, Giannini proved again his inspiring moral leadership because he never stopped believing that San Francisco truly needed honest politicians and reformed laws, especially at the crucial moment of its reconstruction. Soon afterwards, the bipartisan Progressive Republican magnate James Rolph was elected mayor. Even though San Francisco was rebuilt in three years on the basis of its 1847 grid, his most important challenge was to upgrade San Francisco in a grand composition of plazas, boulevards, parks, and public spaces according to the recommendations made by the famous Chicago city planner Daniel Hudson Burnham. The public projects he was particularly involved in were a great new city hall, streetcar tunnels beneath Twin Peaks and Parnassus Heights, an automotive tunnel to unify the city in a north-south direction, and the highway along Ocean Beach.

There is nothing like disaster to bring out the best in human nature. After the devastating Chicago fire of 1871, citizens from around the country sent their carefully saved pennies and dollars. The same instinct was stirred when news of the great 1906 earthquake and fire reached the rest of the world. San Francisco collected large amounts in relief funds and under the leadership of its new and honest mayor James Rolph—re-elected for five consecutive terms—the city could gradually return to its original glory.

Chapter Five

THE DAWN OF BRANCH BANKING

In January 1907, the Bank of Italy was doing very well. Giannini persuaded the board of directors to approve the purchase of an empty lot on the corner of Clay and Montgomery Streets, next to the very heart of the city's financial district but still only a few blocks from North Beach. As was later reported by the *San Francisco Chronicle,* the building in granite and limestone was nine stories high and was "among the most handsome and modern of its kind in the city."[45]

With construction underway, A.P. decided to take a break and have a holiday with Clorinda, their first in fifteen years of marriage. It was a pleasant combination of vacation and business. The Gianninis left San Francisco by train on a journey that included stopovers in Chicago, Pittsburgh, and Philadelphia. After three weeks they arrived in New York, the banking capital of the United States. Even on vacation, he wanted to make the most out of this opportunity and meet other bankers and prominent Italian businessmen. He wanted to learn more about banking outside his native California and go back home with fresh ideas and innovative goals. What he learned instead was that New York's largest banks were short of money and that gold reserves were dangerously low. Unlike paper, gold was a precious metal with significant value and therefore was the most trusted currency at that time. By law, banks were required to keep 25% of their deposits as reserves; the rest could be loaned. However, bankers too often ignored the reserve requirements because granting loans was much more profitable than keeping reserves. In the first scenario, the borrower paid interest to the bank; in the second, it was the bank that had to pay interest to the depositor.

What clearly emerged from all of this was the general weakness of the nation's banking system with its thirty thousand banks, each competitively independent. A powerful central bank that could control the flow of money, as in England, which was then the money center of the world, was missing from the American financial milieu. In London, The Bank of England, the so-called "Old Lady of Threadneedle Street" had invested too much, so its reserves of cash were too low vis-à-vis the amount of money deposited. The "Old Lady" tried to take some corrective measures to make it more difficult to borrow money but it was already too late: the seeds of panic had already been sown.[46] What was happening in London to the Bank of England was happening all over the world including New York and San Francisco. In October 1907, prices on the New York Stock Exchange plummeted. Worried customers tried to withdraw their money. More than 130 banks went bankrupt and riots broke out. The panic even spread west to California. Governor James Gillette declared a bank holiday on October 31, 1907 and some banks started offering paper currency, known also as funny money, instead of the gold they did not have.[47]

Demand for money was slowly rising in San Francisco along with a fall-off in new accounts and deposits. After clearly perceiving a general sense of insecurity, Giannini cut his vacation short. Once at home, his foreboding deepened and he concluded that caution and prudence were the necessary powerful antidotes to the 1907 panic: all the signs were there for those who could read them. He counter-reacted with drastic measures: he cut all the new real estate loans; he started a forceful campaign to increase the Bank's deposits, which proved to be very successful and lucrative; and last but not least, he began rebuilding his reserves of gold. Bank of Italy tellers were instructed to pay out paper money rather than gold. The faith that people had in the Bank, and in Giannini in particular, was so great that these unorthodox moves were accepted without question.[48]

Giannini was thirty-seven when the first local branch bank opened its doors, outside of North Beach, on Mission Street in August 1907. In contrast to most other bankers, his aim was to cater to working people and this time to include a more diverse ethnic clientele, which would go beyond the Italian-American community. He tried hard to adapt to the schedules of his clients, rather than vice versa, an innovation that was entirely unprecedented. The branch was open in the evening and also on Sundays. This brave new undertaking went largely unnoticed and nobody could have ever imagined where it was leading. He was able to turn the financial panic to the advantage of the Bank of Italy. Many banks were forced to suspend gold payments because gold was in short supply. Giannini instead, thanks to his foresight, was able throughout the fifty-day crisis to pay in gold and honor all his commitments, having had the sense to accumulate ample reserves. His bank had a nest egg of about $100,000 above normal requirements and therefore stood out as a sound, exceptionally well-managed institution. Even the respected Crocker-Woolworth National went through a crisis and anxious depositors lined up to withdraw all their funds. At the height of the run, Giannini came to the rescue of his old friend Giacomo Fagan, the Director of an esteemed bank that he felt loyal to, reassuring people that their money was safe and if they brought their Crocker passbooks to the Bank of Italy they would still be honored in gold. At the end of the crisis, every other bank in the city showed heavy declines in assets and deposits while the Bank of Italy sailed through the storm.[49] In December 1907, Bank of Italy assets totaled $2,200,000.

Driven by his curiosity and desire to keep himself and his customers informed, A.P. attended the annual meeting of the California Bankers Association in Pasadena. The topic was how to avoid financial stress. Lyman L. Cage, one of the presenters, was highly impressed by Canada's banking system to the point that Giannini was inspired to visit the country and see for himself. A few months later he also attended the American Bankers Association in Denver. Woodrow Wilson, then the President of Princeton University and future President of the United States, advocated branch banking as a way of preventing banking crises. He pointed out that: "The banks of this country are remote from the people and the people regard them as not belonging to them. If a system of branch banks ... put the resources of the rich banks of the country at the disposal of whole countrysides to whose merchants and farmers only a restricted and local credit is now open, the attitude of plain men everywhere towards the banks and banking would be changed utterly within less than a generation ...."[50]

Wilson's suggestion had strengthened Giannini's new commitment to branch banking. Earlier that year he had taken a three-week trip to eastern Canada and been most impressed by the efficiency of their bank system. In remote places there were branches of the Toronto and Montreal banks that he visited. He saw firsthand that they performed services that no small local bank could have undertaken. From that moment he was convinced that Canada set an example to follow, one that could be as successful in the United States as it had been in Canada for over half a century.

Branch banking is a network of bank offices operating in more than one city or town, locally managed but all under the direction of one Board of Directors and operating with the capital of the whole bank.[51] In the U.S., it was initially attempted in the eighteenth century by the First United States Bank (1791–1811) with eight branches radiating from Philadelphia. Later on from 1816 to 1836, the Second Bank of the United States had twenty-seven branches as far afield as New Orleans and Portland. The result was negative because of the corrupt, inefficient management of the Second Bank, which was compounded by the envy of the other state banks. Moreover, each state had different banking regulations. In England and in Canada on the other hand, branch banking had proven highly successful. Very few branch banks failed, unlike single-unit banks that were isolated and had limited resources.

California would be the ideal state for opening branches of the Bank of Italy, which would offer the services and resources of big-city banks to small communities. If, for example, bad weather caused crops to fail in one area, the bank would divert money from other branches to help. A.P. felt that with honest, efficient management, he could reduce the heavy percentage of bank, commercial, and agricultural failures in California during periods of stress. The expansion of the Bank of Italy did not happen by accident or overnight. A.P. was a hard-working businessman who routinely worked fifteen hours a day and had been convinced, from an early age, that Californians had the richest soil in the world, offering an abundance of fruit, wheat, and vegetables. More clearly than any other banker in his native state, Giannini recognized the confluence of interests between branch banking and California's abundant and varied agricultural economy. According to him, "branch banking will be the steady foundation on which we can build the strongest, happiest, most prosperous state of the Union!"[52] He had already fulfilled his dream by building an earthquake-safe and fireproof bank with a steel structure and huge vaults for the Bank's cash and records, no longer needing to rely on the Crocker-Woolworth for daily deposits. With Florentine architecture, bronze gates, Carrara marble floors, and Italian Renaissance art, his central bank was a symbol of his pride in his Italian heritage. What he could not do without was the open floor plan, with no private offices, which he maintained from his early days at the saloon-bank. He did not want to lose the direct, almost tactile, contact with his clientele. The main hall was a sunny, hospitable place with huge windows and a "cheerful, dependable air" in tune with A.P.'s own disposition, which was always ready to reach out.

It was time now to establish a first out-of-town branch. After cautious and careful planning, Giannini decided on his hometown San Jose in December 1909. The town had grown extensively since he had spent his childhood there; it had developed from a frontier outpost to a major farm center with a population of fifty thousand people, of which thirty thousand were Italian. Most of them worked in growing, packaging, and transporting fruit and vegetables from the fertile farmland close by. The Santa Clara Valley seemed ripe for development and within ten years, California would grow more than two-thirds of the produce in the whole country and San Jose would become the busiest fruit distributing center in the state. A.P. studied the 1909 California

Bank Act and all of its clauses and rather than seeing it as a mere regulatory restraint, he believed it to be an official encouragement to pursue new outlets. Instead of starting a brand-new establishment, he acquired the Commercial and Savings Bank in San Jose, one of the oldest and largest banks in California.

The bank had been founded by wealthy landowners and it paid them large dividends in prosperous times but they lived on borrowed money when times were bad. Small landowners, mostly immigrants, were not welcomed, or totally ignored. The conservative management simply did not understand that the Valley's real wealth was in helping such people.[53] Moreover, the former president had made too many loans to family and friends who failed to pay back the money, threatening the bank's solvency. Ultimately this out-of-touch management and the new California banking laws clashed and the bank was forced to surrender their stocks and seek help from Giannini.

Since the new Bank Act prohibited the Bank of Italy from acquiring stocks directly from the ailing Commercial and Savings, it was a group of individuals representing the Bank who did so, legally assuming all the risk, including his father Scatena, Attilio "Doc" James Bacigalupi, and several others.[54] If they did not have enough cash between them to purchase the shares, they knew that they could count on the Crocker National. The consolidation of the two banks was allowed by law, which was followed by the final step of the liquidation of assets based on a tough and realistic but fair evaluation.[55] This set the pattern for acquisitions for the years to come. Although Giannini had a life-long, semi-antagonistic relationship with his brother Attilio, a San Francisco physician, he appointed him to run the San Jose branch. It was so successful that it ignited a spark in A.P. that was impossible to extinguish. Attilio, a man of unquestionable ability, left his medical practice in 1907 to become part of the Bank of Italy and start a successful financial career. He had graduated from the University of California–Berkeley in medicine, served with some distinction in a field hospital in the Philippines during the Spanish-American War, and started a private practice once he was back in San Francisco. He had received an award for his courage in volunteering to treat patients in a charity hospital during a smallpox epidemic. Attilio thought of himself as a self-made man but had in fact been financially helped with great generosity by his brother A.P., who started working very young, "getting up at midnight and in the early hours of the morning to lay the foundation that made those advantages possible."[56] Attilio frequented the best clubs, impeccably dressed in smart dark suits. In 1909 he married the daughter of a wealthy Los Angeles real estate developer and was thus able to further indulge his expensive tastes. A.P. was gregarious and outgoing, Attilio was distant and a snob. Even though the two brothers were diametrically opposite, they both believed they had found their real vocation in the banking profession. By opening the branch in San Jose, A.P. said later in an interview to the *San Francisco News:* "I saw that we could give better service to everybody. Each branch would be a business-getter for the institution, but each branch likewise would have behind it the resources the bank possessed. We would be able to care for the needs of any customer."[57]

A few years of research and experiment were invested into acquiring knowledge about rural banking before opening another branch in the Santa Clara Valley. By 1910, A.P. had built a network of contacts in the banking world providing valuable and reliable information on the condition of banks in California, especially those that were available for sale. In 1912, he bought another bank in San Mateo where he lived. He preferred once again to acquire an existing institution rather than to start from scratch. He regularly sought the advice of his board, even though most of the time he would conclude that his own plan was the right one. He knew how to involve the people around him and create a motivated working team. In 1913, James and Samuel Fugazi joined the board of directors at the Bank of Italy less than a decade after A.P. had abruptly quit from the board of their father's bank, Columbus Savings and Loan.[58]

He was determined to hire only local staff who truly understood the needs of the community and he would not displace the bank officers that he had bought out. All his employees were required to speak Italian, as he did, and at least one other foreign language. He appointed mostly Italians to his advisory boards but A.P. also made sure that established local families of other backgrounds were involved. He deliberately charged lower interest rates than his competitors. He did not want to repeat the blatant fault he saw in the operation of Canadian branch banks where the managers were almost exclusively sent out from the head offices in major cities and were therefore alien to the townspeople and with no understanding of the potential of the place.[59]

For each new branch, Giannini would personally visit local farmers and townspeople for their feedback and banking needs. He would reach out to minorities other than Italians in California including Russian, Chinese, Yugoslavian, Greek, Mexican, and Portuguese people. As A.P. specified in his advertisement in the *San Jose Mercury and Herald* of November 14, 1909: "The new institution is to pay special attention to the affairs of people who speak English with difficulty and will have employees who speak the French, Italian, Spanish, and Portuguese languages." The new bank was deliberately set up for the "little fellow" who, according to A.P., "is the best customer that a bank can have because he starts with you and stays to the end; whereas the big fellow is only with you so long as he can get something out of you, and when he cannot, he's not for you anymore." It was only when the branch had reached some level of stability and respectability that he would reach out to the established non-foreign-born population.[60] Employees as well as managers worked in the open where it was easy for customers to interact, unlike the tellers in the other banks who would hide behind barred windows to prevent someone from approaching them too closely.

Giannini would conduct a door-to-door campaign with his own sales force, informing them about the new services and possibilities the branch bank would offer in order to get new accounts. They would attend weddings, baptisms, church services, community picnics, and all kinds of social events. This technique proved to be a winning card, as within two years the number of accounts doubled in his San Francisco branches. Once again, he baffled his competitors with his resourceful and imaginative approach, which was based on fulfilling the demands of potential customers from every walk of life. For him, this was not hard work; he truly cherished personal contact and even if he did not succeed in making a new client, he enjoyed the human interaction.

Upon meeting a child saving pennies in an old tomato can, he was inspired to open the School Savings Department, which grew to millions of dollars in deposits. A.P. admitted that even though this was not intended as a profitable enterprise because of the exorbitant administrative expense of such a program, it "puts thrift into the minds of young Americans and that's about the best backlog they can ever own for future security".[61] Learning to manage one's coins in childhood was a quick route to maturity.

He knew that when these children became adults and started earning money, it would be natural for them to place their savings with the Bank of Italy. To A.P., this result was worth the effort because these "seeds" would grow and turn into a fruitful and profitable crop for years to come. Instead of reading books, he was reading people and their needs.

Chapter Six

LOS ANGELES: AN OPPORTUNITY NOT TO BE MISSED

Between 1900 and 1910, the population of San Francisco had increased by 20% while in Los Angeles it had tripled from 100,000 to 320,000. Many people over the age of sixty-five were attracted to the area because of the warm climate, scenery, and lifestyle. In general, this age group had more disposable income and were more inclined to deposit larger amounts of their savings into a bank. In addition, the number of building permits in Los Angeles between 1910 and 1915 was much higher than in San Francisco and bank deposits and loans had doubled.[62] For Giannini, the thriving potential of Los Angeles represented an opportunity that ought not be missed. He had gone to New York for a brief business trip to meet with bankers and noted that almost one million Italian immigrants were living there, but he determined that, for the time being, it was better to concentrate his efforts in his native state. After an extensive tour of southern California in the spring of 1913 with James Fagan, his old friend and mentor, he decided to focus his attention particularly on Los Angeles, an urban settlement in full development. Unlike San Francisco, which was surrounded on three sides by water, Los Angeles could expand in all directions. In 1906, the city annexed a strip of land connecting it to the coast of San Pedro and the Port of Los Angeles was established correcting its previous geographical drawback of being inland with no natural harbor. Moreover, the Los Angeles Aqueduct, completed in 1913, gave adequate water supply to the thirsty city by rerouting annual mountain snowmelt more than two hundred miles across mountains and deserts. Water transformed a desert into a fruitful farmland that supplied tons of citrus fruit and other agricultural commodities.[63]

Oil was discovered in the area in 1909 and Los Angeles was soon producing millions of barrels of oil a year. Many people were attracted to this new urban center in search of steady work and they often needed money to get started.[64] A.P. decided to purchase a small, weak neighbourhood institution called Park Bank, which was in poor financial shape because of careless lending practices and bad investment, and he turned it into a new branch of the Bank of Italy. A.P. was initially seen as an intruder and local bankers felt threatened to the point of suing him. The highly regarded president of Security Trust and Saving, Joseph Sartori, was so angry that he rushed to Sacramento to express his objections and pursued from that moment on a vicious campaign of cutthroat competition. Giannini's opponents were unsuccessful as he proceeded to open three additional branches within a year. This was possible because in giving statutory approval to branch banking, California lawmakers had failed to set any limits on how far any banker could go in opening branches. The state superintendent of banking, William Williams, could do very little to prevent Giannini from moving into Los Angeles.

A.P. could therefore easily pursue his own technique of expansion, which included large-scale advertising, a heavily financed public relations campaign, and the unprecedented fluency of his staff in seven different languages. He placed notices in major dailies announcing the Bank's intention to participate in the urban expansion of Los Angeles, stating "we have money to loan at all times to the man who wishes to build on property that he owns. We have no money for speculators ... we consider the wage earner or small businessman who deposits his savings regularly ... no matter how small the amount may be, to be the most valuable client our bank can have." He would include on his advisory boards presidents of important local companies and banks, who proved to become a rapidly expanding expert network, instrumental in formulating new commercial ventures.

Unfortunately, A.P. would learn the hard way that southern California was very different from the north. His previously winning advertising strategy proved not to have the same impact and the new branches were incurring losses. Most newcomers to Los Angeles were native midwestern farmers "who came with no funds or prospects ... apparently trusting that heaven would provide them ... They camped on the outskirts of town, and their camps became suburbs."[65]

In 1910, 53% of the people living there were of native-born parentage, white and Protestant, compared to only 28% in San Francisco. Los Angeles was one of the least diverse cities in California. The arrival of an Italian Catholic from a rival city did not inspire the confidence and eventually the gratitude that it had among the ethnic neighborhoods of San Francisco. Rumors circulated that doing business with the Bank of Italy was risky and unpatriotic. The usual false speculations about A.P. working with the Pope or the Mafia resurfaced. The headlines of major newspapers proclaimed "Italians Take Over Park Bank"; this bald statement revealed not only derision but also racial intolerance, if not outright xenophobic indignation.[66] Moreover, Los

Angeles already had thirty-nine banks, foremost among them the "Big Seven,"[67] including Security Trust and Savings with resources of approximately $50 million—nearly four times the size of the Bank of Italy. Los Angeles did not need another one and therefore did not welcome it. At the time, Los Angeles had a relatively small Italian population: 3,802 compared to the 16,918 of San Francisco. Giannini was almost defeated by the persistent hostile machinations all around him in Los Angeles, and several directors of the San Francisco headquarters opposed his expansionist policy. Realizing that his board had lost confidence, in December 1913 A.P. threatened to retire and pay back the bank's losses, assuming full responsibility. What was at stake was not only the Bank of Italy's prestige but the key to the development of branch banking in the state. After assuming personal control over the branch and working frantically over the next several months with the help of his loyal North Beach veteran Pedrini, he devised an aggressive strategy to acquire new customers. He gradually removed all the dissidents from the board and instead of giving up on Los Angeles, he moved the bank from a peripheral location to a more prominent, permanent address at Seventh and Broadway, at the very heart of the downtown shopping district. He paid four times as much rent for this new location because he wanted to prove he was there to stay. The board was very impressed by his confidence and determination and unanimously rejected his resignation by voting to support his daring plan. Moreover, the economic conditions of California, after a dismal temporary slump, improved rapidly because the World War I was creating new markets for shipbuilders, small manufacturers, and farmers who needed more and more credit to buy specialized machinery and hire large numbers of field workers. In 1916, the second full year of the war, the combined value of

California field crops, fruits, vegetables, poultry, and livestock jumped to $664 million, a staggering increase over previous years.[68]

In most areas, farmers had to pay high interest rates—up to 12% in remote farm towns—and in many cases were compelled to pay a bonus to brokers. There were many banks that would turn down requests for loans from small borrowers to finance their investments in machinery as well as property; they would instead pass the property on to a broker who charged from 2% to 5% for his services. "Besides the mortgage, the farmer had to pay an interest rate of 8% or more, and from three to five times the actual cost of sending a man to appraise the property."[69]

A.P.'s vision of branch banking always reflected a genuine concern for the small borrower and the conviction that high interest rates were ruinous to the farmers. Given his insight that large profits were to be made through quantity as well as quality, his emphasis on low interest rates fit well with his business scheme. Giannini lowered the standard rate of interest on loans in all the towns where he established branches of his bank; he offered two, three, and even five percentage points lower than what other banks were then charging. He pursued a policy—unusual for a businessman—of cutting down on the amount of money the bank would make in order to help his clients. He emphasized an egalitarian approach to the bank's lending operations.[70] This philosophy included free advice offered to customers in any number of areas, teaching people how to expand their business and make more money. He was inspired during the war years to continue his expansion and moved quickly, establishing eight new branches in urban centers and ten in the untapped, rural communities of the San Joaquin Valley, the largest and richest of California's agricultural regions, spanning from San Francisco to Los Angeles. Farmers and ranchers saw that they could afford to borrow money for the first time and the rural press praised Giannini's unprecedentedly liberal lending policy.

In a single decade, he successfully built a state-wide system of branch banks that paid the most impressive dividends. Annual profits from the Fresno branch went from $9,449 to $104,515 while the annual earnings from its Stockton branch went from $23,000 to $132,000 in just three years.[71]

Branch banking was still a contentious matter; in fact, in 1916 the American Bankers Association had actually condemned it; since 1909 nine states had prohibited the system, twenty-seven were silent on the matter as it had yet to affect them, and only twelve states had laws that permitted the practice. In addition, restrictions and continual new state regulations upon bankers made it increasingly harder to expand and profit under this system. One of the new policies was that no bank could carry real estate—property it had acquired by trade, purchase, or foreclosure—on its books for longer than five years. To get around this situation, Giannini formed the Stockholder's Auxiliary Corporation, which was owned by the Bank of Italy stockholders in proportion to their Bank of Italy holdings. This corporation was a legally separate entity, independent of the bank, and could buy, hold, or sell stocks and properties as well as banks.[72] Interestingly enough, it was William Williams, the state superintendent of banking, who had kindly suggested the holding company device to him, and indeed the Stockholder's Auxiliary provided Giannini with the solution he had been looking for.

The exponential growth of Giannini's banking network frightened and surprised the smaller bankers, steadily creating ranks of powerful enemies, as well as some allies. By 1918, the Bank of Italy was the fourth-largest bank in California and the first state-wide branch bank in the country; moreover, its total resources had climbed from $22 million to $100 million.[73]

A.P. designed an extremely flexible and democratic system according to which each branch would be primarily sensitive to the seasonal needs of the region and respond quickly to any emergency. A small but prosperous agricultural town north of San Francisco, Santa Rosa, had a history of bank failures due to mismanagement. The branch of the Bank of Italy was, however, very stable and yet a run occurred in a curious manner. A laundry driver spread a rumor that the branch was in trouble. This was apparently confirmed by the fact that the Santa Rosa branch was closed for one hour for the funeral of the mayor. On the basis of this misunderstanding, the townspeople panicked and by the next morning the bank was virtually under siege by alarmed customers and the manager, Glen Murdock, who had only $50,000 to cover $3,000,000 in deposits, was in real trouble. He hastily appealed to the Bank of Italy branches in nearby towns, which provided another $400,000 but this was not enough and he decided at last to call the main office.

The whole situation was rescued by Scatena who promptly brought $500,000 mostly in gold and silver and, to everyone's surprise, by A.P. Giannini himself the following day, with another $3,000,000 in gold. Giannini re-enacted what the Jewish businessman Isaias Hellman, President of the Nevada Bank, and Chairman of Columbus Savings and Loan Society, San Francisco, had done years before in Los Angeles during a similar run. He started to heap mounds of gold coins on the counter, in plain sight of the worried customers. Giannini had brought a large amount from his personal account in San Francisco and all those coins soon became towering stacks of gold, a testament to the financial strength of the Bank of Italy. The sight of all that shiny metal was a tonic. As the frantic crowd watched the golden towers grow, panic subsided. Many customers re-deposited the funds they had withdrawn in their earlier frenzy. By the end of the day, the coffers of the branch were replenished.[74] The run stopped only because of the quick shipments of cash from the central headquarters of San Francisco. A unit or stand-alone bank surely would have collapsed under the financial pressure. Only the enormous resources behind the little Santa Rosa branch had saved the day.[75] This specific run shows how branch banking was the antidote to an emergency that otherwise would have obliterated the financial institution altogether. Moreover, the global scale of A.P.'s ambitions did not stop, in spite of the Bank of Italy's slightly tarnished reputation and the damaging schemes of his enemies—whom he held personally responsible for the Santa Rosa run and actually became more evident in the postwar era (1919–1921). In 1919, he purchased the East River National Bank in New York as his first eastern outpost and within a year he also bought a medium-sized bank in Naples, Italy, called the Banca dell'Italia Meridionale, (the name was later changed to *Banca d'America e d'Italia*), which gave him a direct branch outlet in Europe. To manage the East River National he appointed his brother Attilio, and to solve the issues of the Neapolitan Bank he had Pedrini fire most of the bank's executives for their incompetence and greed and introduced efficient management, which immediately gave excellent results. This way Giannini laid the promising foundations for an intercontinental network of banks expanding across the Atlantic.

Chapter Seven

THE LARGEST BANK WEST OF CHICAGO

In 1921, the headquarters of the Bank of Italy moved from Clay and Montgomery Streets, where they had occupied only the bottom floor, to a shining white granite seven-story building at One Powell Street, where every floor was occupied by the bank in the heart of the financial district. At this point, the Bank of Italy had the largest bank building in the country. Every aspect was calculated to make banking faster, simpler, more comfortable, and accessible.

Giannini became aware of the new role that women were playing in household financial matters. After decades of petitions, women had finally won the right to vote in 1920; before then, they had no right to buy and sell property and therefore they were inevitably dependent on their husbands, brothers, or fathers and had no legal voice in government. In that same year, Giannini lost his mother and mentor, Virginia Scatena, who had proved to be the pivotal figure in the most important financial decisions that directly led to the prosperity of their family. On June 27, 1921, A.P. established a department devoted exclusively to women, a revolutionary idea meant to promote their economic independence. The opening celebrations lasted for three days. The entire top floor of the building was the headquarters of the Women's Bank, where they could conduct banking business without any interference, in a beautifully decorated environment, filled with all kinds of flowers.

A.P. appointed a woman to manage the Women's Bank, and customers were welcomed by an entirely female staff. They were instructed to patiently teach customers how to write checks and, if they were not able to write, how to sign their names with thumbprints. The bank, the only one in America of this kind, offered a full range of services to help women save, borrow, and invest wisely. Staff members conducted free evening classes to teach women about business and money matters.[76] After two years, the revolutionary Women's Bank, which reflected a necessary social change, had more than ten thousand customers, $1,500,000 in deposits, and over $5,000,000 in transactions.[77] The Women's Bank proved so successful that Giannini opened a second branch in Los Angeles. Women's organizations throughout the country praised this pioneering enterprise and Giannini's forward thinking.

The Women's Bank was not the only noteworthy aspect of the new Bank of Italy; another very important feature was the vault itself: it was made of steel and concrete, weighed fifty tons, and became the showpiece of the grand opening attended by thousands of people.

A.P. had no private office, no personal secretary, and answered his own phone. He wanted to be accessible to any customer who wanted to see him. He perpetuated his long-standing philosophy of insisting that stock should be widely distributed among customers, with an average of about twenty shares, thus keeping ownership in the hands of many people who would come to regard the bank as a friendly institution in which they were personally invested. A.P. never permitted wealthy clients to buy heavily, a practice that, more than any other, would leave his competitors dumbfounded.

With two hundred thousand depositors, A.P. had built the largest bank west of Chicago. However, he did not want his success to alienate the fishermen and dockworkers of North Beach, who had been his long-time clients. He had serious qualms about having moved away from his roots in San Francisco's Italian community and his own humble origins. For this reason, he was determined to honor his past and decided to bring some of North Beach downtown to the financial district by including his father as Chairman of the Board and Armando Pedrini, the bank's first cashier, as the vice president.

These doubts did not prevent him from aspiring to further expansion. He planned to expand into the city of Sacramento, the capital of California, about eighty miles northeast of San Francisco. Information of his future plans reached the ears of Sacramento competitors who organized a whispering campaign designed to mobilize public opinion against the threat of the Bank of Italy, hinting that it was undemocratic, un-American, and unsafe. They spent quite some time at the state capital urging legislators to limit the Bank of Italy's growth. Independent bankers had every reason to fear A.P. because he was uncommonly persistent.

Sometimes owners of struggling banks asked A.P. to buy them out so they could avoid the scandal of business failure; other times he would approach owners and offer to buy their banks. If faced with resistance, A.P. would either offer more money or resort to ingenious techniques. More than once, when the owner was reluctant to sell, A.P. would have an assistant to get out of the car in front of the potential new branch, as if measuring distances with his feet. When the owner noticed this odd behavior, he would inquire what was going on, to which the assistant would reply that the Bank of Italy was planning to open a branch at the opposite corner; this would usually change the owner's mind as there was no way to directly compete with the economic strength of the Bank of Italy.[78] A.P.'s personality was persuasive, forceful, and at times intimidating. Others could no longer compete with the Bank of Italy because it had grown so large and powerful. Forty-one outlets gave him resources that very few, if any, could match, but A.P. always prioritized the ethnic minorities in every community and prided himself on the bank's valuable and unique customer service.

Being a born fighter, Giannini confronted the opposition of the local banking community by initiating a counter-campaign. He dispatched twenty-nine employees from the central head-quarters to solicit signatures of local citizens desiring a branch. Over eight thousand signatures were collected urging the bank superintendent to issue a permit. Superintendent Charles Stern had discriminated against him, routinely rejecting his permit applications because he was heavily influenced by the competition and felt an acute disdain for branch banking which, he thought, was Canadian and European in principle and not suited to the temperament of the American people. Moreover, it was seen as essentially monopolistic and threatened the American way of banking. However, Stern had badly underestimated A.P., who all the same acquired a number of branches through the Stockholder's Auxiliary Corporation he had founded, circumventing the superintendent's restraints. There was, according to A.P., always a way to move ahead.

The regulatory restrictions were dictated by spite against him personally rather than the ever-increasing spread of branch banking. Stern had first rejected an application to open a branch in Sacramento but just two weeks after Jonathan Dodge, a prominent Los Angeles attorney and former banker, assumed the superintendent's office in June 1921, he approved the request without hesitation. In July of the same year, he granted three additional branches to the Bank of Italy. Giannini had gone personally to Sacramento, helped finance a city filtration plant, and managed to convince Dodge of the beneficial impact that a Bank of Italy branch would have on the local community.

A.P. had already determined that the ideal manager of the new Sacramento branch would be John S. Chambers, former comptroller of the state of California. Chambers had charm, ability, and the necessary local connections. Five days after Dodge granted the permit, the Bank of Italy was in full operation in California's capital city.

Giannini, with his volcanic temperament, was perhaps working too fast. Dodge started looking into the Bank of Italy operations after the complaints of some independent bankers, and he actually found that the accounting department was often behind in documenting recent acquisitions and that new branches were frequently unsupervised for months at a time because the main office had other, more pressing concerns. Dodge was worried that Giannini was behaving as a *pater familias* and the Bank of Italy was becoming a "one-man bank." As a consequence, Dodge refused to grant further permits for new branches until A.P. corrected these existing issues. A.P. was especially dismayed because these accusations alerted John Perrin, the chairman of the Federal Reserve Bank of San Francisco as well as the Federal Reserve Board in Washington, which threatened to tarnish the reputation of his bank.

When the head office of the Bank of Italy moved to Powell Street, Giannini closed his Market Street branch, which was only a block away, and to avoid further applications he decided to open the new Liberty Bank with a national rather than a state charter, a loophole that would not require further permission. A.P. had now devised intricate legal methods to bypass state banking superintendents that he would develop extensively throughout the decade. John Perrin was furious at the somewhat devious maneuver.

Moreover, when A.P. decided to organize the new Liberty Bank as an independent state-chartered institution rather than a branch, Perrin was irritated even further. A.P. brought the Bank of Italy under the banner of the Federal Reserve System in 1919 and he thought that, by having reached an agreement with the Federal Reserve officials, he could proceed with his expansion plans without any interference. Instead on July 11, 1921, he received an intimidating note from Perrin, who officially demanded a change in policy invoking a strict ban on the expansion on any bank in the Federal Reserve system outside the headquarters city of such a bank, "except in great emergency."

The Liberty Bank, destined to spectacular growth, was to Perrin a golden pain in the neck.[79] Giannini was confronted by a growing number of opponents including bank officials, politicians, and members of the Federal Reserve Board as well as unprecedented animosity at the state and federal levels towards the largest branch banking organization in America. To mitigate this double act of defiance towards the Federal Reserve System, A.P. strategically hired a public official for his new bank and—given his political influence—William Gibbs McAdoo, the son-in-law of Woodrow Wilson and former Secretary of the Treasury under Wilson, managed to smooth out the existing controversy and negotiate an agreement. The Federal Reserve Board would grant licenses to more than two dozen branches A.P. had bought in the previous two years, on condition that he would promise to ask for their approval for new branches in the future, and declare the maximum number of branches the Bank of Italy intended to have. In a surprising move, A.P. avoided direct confrontation and responded by sailing off to Europe for a year and telling his colleagues and subordinates: "If you can't do a thing one way, you do it another way." Before leaving, as a remarkable entrepreneur and effective manager, he made plans to increase the paid-up capital by $5,000,000, the largest sum to date that the bank had attempted to raise at one time.

He declared that he did not intend to communicate with the bank or any bank official for the whole year, nor did he wish to receive any information or give any orders. He wanted to prove to his enemies and his staff alike that the Bank of Italy was capable of pushing ahead without its founder at the wheel. By Independence Day 1922, the $5,000,000 increase in capital was all paid and the Bank of Italy was in excellent condition as regards profits, loans, and liquidity. However, Perrin and Dodge jointly made every effort to discredit and sabotage the bank by hinting at inadequate management and "unbridled disrespect for authority," while granting multiple permits to Giannini's competitors.

The fight against the bank was getting out of hand. On April 18, 1922, the Federal Reserve Board sent two of its ranking members to the Federal Reserve Bank of San Francisco for a thorough investigation on the whole issue of branch banking in view of reaching the precise goal of limiting its future expansion. A draft agreement was presented but nobody signed it. Moreover, the executive committee of the Bank of Italy was summoned. The permits to incorporate new banks had been withheld by Dodge because of his own objections. The day after that special inquisition-like hearing, the five banks received the okay from Dodge on the recommendation of the same two supervisors. It was a great victory for A.P.'s employees to have accomplished this while their boss was away in Europe, thus solidifying Giannini's firm conviction that the Bank of Italy was not a "one-man show," but rather a mature, responsible financial institution.

When A.P. returned in the spring of 1923 he found a job well done. Moreover, Jonathan Dodge had been replaced by John F. Johnson as superintendent of banking, and seemed willing to establish a more cooperative relationship.

Therefore Giannini was ready for a challenging new expansionistic campaign, first moving into San Luis Obispo, a farm town located among rolling hills, about 250 miles south of San Francisco. The prospect that the Bank of Italy was assuming a larger presence in the southern part of the state by acquiring the local Union National Bank provoked acrimonious opposition from his banking rivals. When a team of the Bank of Italy arrived in town, its windows were broken, office furniture smashed, and books and records were pulled out of file cabinets and strewn about. In spite of other organized protest meetings and damaging accusations, in 1923 A.P. was also granted a *de novo* permit by Johnson to open a branch sixty miles to the south, in Santa Maria, whose fertile valley of dairy and sugar beet farms had attracted a conspicuous number of Swiss, Italian, and Portuguese immigrants. The permit, however, was later revoked on the basis of the ruthless tactics alleged to have been adopted by his collaborators in an overly ambitious approach.

Sometimes Giannini was taken too literally by his Italian collaborators, who were often described as "missionaries" since the early 1920s, when the Bank of Italy emerged as a powerful force in the state. Given the fact that most banks usually ignored minorities, in part because of language barriers, he wisely and innovatively established himself as an honest and generous intermediary. Driven by his life-long conviction that immigrants generated more business than the native-born, he kept to his policy of establishing separate ethnic divisions of the bank, including Greek, Russian, Slavic, Portuguese, Latin American, Spanish, and Chinese. The largest was the Italian department, under the direction of Armando Pedrini, sharing responsibilities and duties with Robert Paganini. "Giannini's crusaders" as they were also called, were all Italian and their main goal was to spread the gospel of the first democratic, cosmopolitan, and progressive bank of the people, and turn every Italian resident of California into a depositor and a stockholder of the Bank of Italy. They had spread across the hinterland of San Francisco and gradually the whole state of California with messianic dedication. They were intended at the beginning as a promotional arm of the bank but soon became a voluntary social service agency, well known for their free services. They helped Italian immigrants become American citizens, offering complimentary evening classes to prepare them for their examinations. They also helped Russian immigrants fleeing the Red regime by preparing the necessary documents. They primarily provided access to credit but also assisted in finding jobs for the unemployed, translated official documents into different languages, visited the sick, and helped the needy to buy food and other essential items.

Giannini was a man driven by results and he demanded daily reports. Less than five years after the department began operations, forty thousand Italians had become Bank of Italy depositors, a figure that corresponded to 20% of the total number, while a far higher percentage (40%) became stockholders, most of whom were living in California.[80] A.P.'s main goal to disseminate his bank's stock was pursued because his business philosophy was based on the principle of attracting a mass rather than a class market. It bred a feeling of loyalty and a sense of community amongst tens of thousands of small depositors who considered their branches as handy neighborhood banks rather than units of intimidating national banking giants. Giannini in his clairvoyance had also created a business advisory service, providing free guidance and advice for a wide range of small-business enterprises, particularly in the diversification of Californian agriculture. He was able to expand available credit through the Federal Reserve Board, greatly enlarging his lending capacity. As the *San Francisco Bulletin* commented: "The crops have been moved with the assistance of straight bank loans." By the use of such devices, A.P. was able to cushion the credit crises of major farm groups such as the California Apricot and Prune Growers Association or the California Bean Growers Association. Unlike other institutions, his was able to weather a succession of farm crises without serious losses and to establish itself as the dominant purveyor of farm credit in California in the 1920s, including in newly emerging industries like cotton. World War I had greatly stimulated the development of large-scale cotton culture in California, and Giannini, having initially financed it only cautiously, ended up supporting fully one half of the state's cotton crop. Besides being the major supporter of the state's booming agribusiness, he cautiously endorsed expansion in home and small-business loans in the growing consumer market in appliances and cars. He even created a motion-picture loan division, which eventually helped renowned actors and directors such as Mary Pickford, Charlie Chaplin, Douglas Fairbanks, and D.W. Griffith establish United Artists. In this way, A.P. explored indiscriminately all the untapped potential that California had to offer.

Chapter Eight

CELEBRATING TWENTY YEARS OF
TENACIOUS EXPANSION

What Giannini called his "baby bank" was now approaching its twentieth anniversary and he intended to turn this event into a milestone. The date was set: October 17, 1924. It had proved to be a very democratic institution serving the public at large, and in particular the people from different ethnic backgrounds who previously had no bank at all, or who had been refused by other financial institutions. In spite of the attacks of his competitors, on any given day the Bank of Italy and its branches counted among their customers butchers, bakers, loggers, fishermen, farmers, and viticulturists, to name but a few. No one was ignored, and A.P. insisted that all be treated courteously and with the utmost attention.

It was structured as a welcoming big extended family rather than as an octopus spreading its tentacles, as his enemies would maliciously maintain. A few of the original founders of the bank were still active: his stepfather Scatena served as chairman of the board while his brothers George and Attilio were active parts of the team. George, who by now headed L. Scatena & Co., was one of the bank directors and Attilio was in New York, managing the East River National Bank with great success. Key associates were still vice president Armando Pedrini, his first employee, and Cobb Hale, a mature and distinguished merchant of old Yankee lineage who proved crucial to the expanding policy of bank purchases for almost two decades. A.P. was well aware that a Catholic man of Italian-American background with a foreign-sounding name could not have secured the same results. He had not forgotten the lessons he had learned from his father in the produce commission days. His aspiration in fact was to ultimately leave control of the bank in the hands of its employees—the men and women who built and operated it—a concept that was radically pioneering, to say the least.

He introduced a sweeping new plan whereby 40% of the bank's net earnings were set aside for its personnel. This was to cover bonuses and the purchase of stock in the company. A.P. also introduced a rule according to which the president of the bank could not hold that position for longer than five years.

To further demonstrate that the Bank of Italy was a fully developed, responsible financial institution, and not a one-man operation, Giannini unexpectedly decided to announce his retirement as president and serve only as chairman of the Advisory Committee. The new president was the tough young lawyer James A. Bacigalupi and all the others would be promoted one step higher. This decision underlined once more his selfless nature; he wanted to be free to concentrate on major policies and prove at the same time that "his boys and girls" were coming along satisfactorily, and he truly derived great pleasure in seeing their development. Later on in life he admitted, "I have worked without thinking of myself. This is the largest factor in whatever success I have attained."

A.P. was fortunate to be able to gradually but steadily count on Mario, his eldest son, who in spite of his poor health—he had haemophilia—proved to be an invaluable asset. Since childhood, Mario had the ambition to become a banker like his father. He began to work as a clearing and distributing clerk at the bank while still in high school. After attending the University of California at Berkeley and graduating from its law school in 1920, Mario joined the bank on a full-time basis. He was not treated in any special way but actually had to work harder than any other employee. He climbed the Bank of Italy ladder on the basis of his own merit. Virgil, his brother, who was six years younger, displayed an exceptional talent for public relations that he successfully put to use, interacting with other banks and institutions. It was Mario who showed a sense of leadership and total command of financial matters. In the personnel department, to which he was transferred, he displayed a particular ability to understand the problems of the bank's employees. He became assistant to the president after returning from Italy, where he gained international experience working at the local *Banca d'America e d'Italia*. Mario was so innovative that he founded the Bankamerica Club for athletic and social activities and the "Suggestion Committee" in which any employee could come up with a constructive idea to be brought to the immediate attention of the bank's top executives.

During this period, the agitation about branch banking continued but the economic conditions in California worked in A.P.'s favor. In 1924, the collapse of the Valley Bank of Fresno with its eight branches turned out to be an extraordinary opportunity for Giannini. The State Superintendent of Banking, J. Franklin Johnson, and the Federal Reserve Board specifically asked the Bank of Italy and the Pacific Southwest Bank, two of the strongest banks in the state, to absorb the failing Valley Bank in Fresno to protect the depositors. The bank had been opened in 1921 by W.D. Mitchell, a butcher, who turned into a small-town banker and started a local branch system, trying to follow the example of Giannini, hoping to achieve the same prosperity. He ventured into speculative and unsecured loans and the Valley Bank expanded into several vineyard towns, but after three years of operation it was in serious trouble and ultimately Mitchell ended up in jail. Giannini was urged to intervene. He was reluctant to do so, but in this way he acquired an important political advantage since the institutions were now willing to suspend their earlier restrictions on the extension of his branches.[81]

A.P. developed additional strategies to facilitate his program of expansion, adhering to his lifelong vision of an effective mix between centralization at headquarters and decentralization in sub-regions and branches. He also found a clever system to circumvent the obstacles preventing him from expanding southward. For three years in a row, his Los Angeles competitors managed to persuade three consecutive superintendents that branch banking in the south should be limited to southern bankers only. This clearly privileged Joseph Sartori, one of his powerful rivals, and other local branch bankers.

In 1919, A.P. had formed a new holding company called the Bancitaly Corporation, designed to gradually become the principal instrument for the purchase of additional banks. This was, to begin with, a small corporation that owned the majority of the stocks of the East River National in New York City and of the *Banca d'America e d'Italia* in Italy. Legally, it was a separate entity that functioned in a similar way to the Auxiliary Stockholder's Corporation vis-à-vis the Bank of Italy and could easily get around the federal government's continuing prohibition of branch banking across state lines. It increasingly turned into an

investment trust rather than a mere holding company and purchased stocks in other banks in the United States and some of
the leading banks in Europe as well as in industrial corporations.
It invested heavily in the Bank of Italy; the latter's stockholders
reciprocally owned 90% of Bancitaly's stock because by establishing this close relationship, Giannini's intention was to keep it
deliberately away from speculators. Moreover, Bancitaly profits
went from $1,216,000 in 1924 to $4,556,000 in 1925, and to
$11,000,000 in 1926.[82]

Giannini's next move was then to transfer the Bancitaly headquarters to Los Angeles and buy more than two dozen
banks, of which eleven were actually in the city. And to further
underline his intentions, he opened a twelve-story Bank of Italy
building in the heart of downtown Los Angeles. A.P. had arrived
prominently in southern California and was there to stay once
and for all.

Giannini believed with all his heart that branch banking
was good for the country, to serve under-represented people,
and that the day was coming for it to be widely accepted. Unlike chain banking where each bank, in spite of common ownership, was a separate corporation that offered limited amounts
on loans, branch banking proved to be much more useful because each branch could count on the resources of the entire
system. A.P. had invested under difficult circumstances in this
endeavor ever since August 1907 when he opened his first
branch at 3343 Mission Street, San Francisco, using the Bank
of Italy's increasing deposits to expand beyond North Beach.
However, given the constant machinations of the small independent bankers and anti-branch banking opponents as well
as the persistent prejudices and abuse of discretionary power

on the part of several superintendents, he decided to further extend his alternative strategies.

In 1924, he bought The Bank of America, one of the most prominent state-chartered banks in Los Angeles and reached a special agreement with its president, Orra Monette. A.P. would not hold any office in the financial institution but Bancitaly would own all of its stocks and operate as its subsidiary. During the same year, he felt confident enough to ask Johnson, the State Superintendent of Banks, for free access to the establishment of new branches since he had issued fifty-four permits between 1923 and 1925 to A.P.'s competitors and only one to him.

Johnson clearly wanted to block Bank of Italy's advance outside the northern part of the state, making it a monopoly issue. However, California banking laws did not specifically prohibit a bank in one part of the state from opening a branch in another. Johnson was clearly exceeding his authority. A.P. felt discriminated against, especially after a further denial to relocate a branch in Los Angeles, only a few blocks north of where it had previously been, in the hub of an old Italian neighborhood.

A.P. was so insulted that he decided to contest the decision by applying to the California Supreme Court, but with no luck. In addition, he had asked the superintendent to allow him to consolidate his four separate branch-banking systems. These included the Liberty Bank of San Francisco, the Bank of America in Los Angeles, the Commercial National Trust and Savings Bank of Los Angeles, and the Bank of Italy. His major objective had been the merger of Bank of Italy and all his subsidiary state-chartered banks into a unified, statewide branch banking system.

In order to unite all four banks, it was necessary to acquire the approval respectively of the Federal Reserve Board and the

California State banking superintendent. He applied and received a seventeen-page letter of concern. A reply from A.P.'s office of fifty-eight pages failed to convince the superintendent. Giannini and his staff were at first incredulous and then, as a last resort, decided to fight by taking direct part in the gubernatorial election of the state, supporting Progressive Republican Lieutenant Governor C.C. Young who, thanks to Giannini's campaigning, won the nomination by a landslide of 12,000 votes. In the hope of balanced and fair treatment, his intervention through his executives, employees, and stockholders proved necessary because the existence and future growth of the Bank of Italy were at stake.

The successful last-minute blitz campaign from Oregon to the Mexican border was unfavorably reported on by *The Los Angeles Times*: "California does not need a Mussolini, financial, political, or otherwise." Over the years, however, Giannini maintained a dignified silence in the face of the anti-Italian prejudice he encountered throughout his banking career. A.P.'s involvement in politics was never by choice but only by necessity, when major obstacles prevented him from pursuing the best interests of his customers.

His massive expansion was finally consolidated on January 26, 1927.[83] This was possible thanks to the open-minded attitude of Superintendent Will C. Wood (who succeeded Johnson) after California's Governor-elect Young took office. He was a popular and progressive educator who had resigned from California's school system and was totally unbiased vis-à-vis branch banking. After a week in office, he approved the merger of the four Giannini banking systems under the name of Liberty Bank of America, because he believed that this would be of advantage to the community. He stated in an interview with the *San Fran-*

cisco Examiner that "it is neither good banking nor good public policy to keep banks separate in operation when the ownership is practically identical."[84]

Undoubtedly Giannini's belated and reluctant intervention was decisive; it proved a great success by removing all the impediments to his consolidation efforts.[85] He had been fighting on two fronts at the same time: at the state level against the opposition to statewide branches and at the national level since Washington was clearly still in favor of curbing branch banking. A new bill concerning the regulation of banks was in the making for a year and a half under the name of the McFadden Act; it offered alternatives to this crucial issue.

Congressman McFadden, a successful banker himself, believed in branch banking. Many California bankers endorsed the bill with the exception of Section 9 concerning branch-banking restrictions and the so-called Hull amendments, aiming at preventing branch banking in twenty-eight states. Senator Carter Glass of Virginia was in favor of branch banking and so was the new Comptroller of the Currency, Joseph W. McIntosh. After various attempts, in December 1926, McFadden re-proposed his bill, but without the Hull amendments and with a major improvement, requested by Senator Glass, which allowed national or state banks to keep any branch or branches they had in operation on the date the bill became law. Giannini had already envisioned a way to reach his ultimate cross-state goal.

By setting up the Bank of America of Los Angeles and the Commercial National he overcame the zoning banking limitations enforced by Johnson, and acquired branches otherwise forbidden to the Bank of Italy in the south. In the same way, through the Liberty Bank in San Francisco owned by Bancitaly he started a successful strategy of expanding to the north, acquiring in the summer of 1925 twelve branches in remote places, especially in mining towns and timber communities, and in the fall, three more banks in the Sacramento Valley.

Giannini was farsighted enough to clarify Section 9 directly with Charles W. Collins, the Deputy Comptroller of the Currency, who had collaborated in writing the McFadden Act and had followed its long course through Congress. When he learned for sure that a national bank could absorb another bank provided both parties had head offices and branches in the same cities, he bought a number of banks faster than before, thanks to the exceptional profits made by the Bancitaly Corporation.

On February 25, 1927, Giannini achieved complete victory with the passage of the McFadden Bill in the U.S. Senate. With the merger of the Bank of Italy and the Liberty Bank of America just a few days earlier, all his controversial banks were finally consolidated into one giant: the Bank of Italy National Trust and Savings Association. It was now a national bank, subject to federal, not state, regulation and included 276 branches in 199 localities, with deposits of $616,000,000. This made it the largest bank in the West and the third-largest bank in the country, after the National City Bank and the Chase National, both in New York.[86] Since 1920, he had been forced to embark on a relentless battle to keep alive his progressive idea of banking, but his perseverance had paid off. His victory was due not only to his talent and to the support of the best banking experts he could count on at different levels, but also to the personal loyalty of the millions of grateful customers of the Bank of Italy. "His victory was more than a victory for the Bank of Italy. A.P. Giannini and his allies had changed the course of banking in the United States, and changed it for the better."[87]

Giannini was a dynamic man, a visionary thinker, an experimenter, and a risk-taker. He wanted to be the first to use innovative ideas and daring lines of action, fight widely held stereotypes, and build a new image of the Italian immigrant as being worthy of respect. Perhaps having been born into a family of farmers gave him a practical pioneer's mentality; he knew that to cling tenaciously to tradition—no matter how much one loved it—was only to encourage stasis rather than progress. He was consistently challenging himself and dreaming new dreams. After building the largest network of interrelated banks in the West in less than two decades he was ready to conquer new frontiers.

If branches could operate so successfully in California, why not on a nationwide scale?

His goal was to expand his empire from coast to coast and eventually across the continent. It was hard to believe that American banks were allowed, under the existing laws, to establish branches and operate them in foreign countries but not in other American states. To correct this blatant contradiction, A.P. started a new lobbying campaign in Congress for an amendment to the McFadden Act that would allow branch banking on a national scale.

In 1928, Giannini merged the Bank of Italy with the Bank of America, Los Angeles, to create what would become the largest state-chartered banking institution in the country. Everybody realized by then that he was an honest far-sighted banker who had built one of the largest financial empires in the United States and become a major force in American banking, thanks to his extraordinary profile as entrepreneur, manager, and taskmaster.

Many Californians, particularly Italian-Americans, took pride in his accomplishments knowing that it brought them a certain respectability that society at large had withheld from them. One told a reporter: "Before Giannini, I was a *dago*. Now I am an American."[88] Giannini's reputation was soaring and he was included among the most respected self-made Italian-Americans who shaped the cultural landscape of California and the modern West, along with Marco Fontana, Antonio Cerruti, and Domenico Ghirardelli, to name just a few. Cerruti and Fontana came from Liguria and established a chain of canneries under the Del Monte label. Most of their workers were Italian and their cannery soon became the largest in the world. Domenico Ghirardelli was another enterprising Italian who settled in San Francisco after the Gold Rush and founded the Ghirardelli chocolate empire with Italian immigrant labor, at the site of what is now called Ghirardelli Square.

Giannini's stature was even higher, thanks to his vision and generosity; his meteoric rise was compared to the Rothschilds and the Morgans but, unlike them, he was the first financier, according to the *San Francisco Examiner,* "to make banking and investments a huge democratic fraternity."[89] This concept was radical, to say the least, and became his unique mark of distinction to the very end. He used to say in all honesty, "I have no sympathy for the man who lives to make money. There may be pleasure in the game for some, but how futile!"

Although he had a profound respect for hard cash, he considered the banking business not an end in itself as a mere road to wealth, but a tool to reach higher personal and societal goals. Since 1920, Giannini's salary had been $50,000 a year, which was very low for the head of an institution as large and rich as the Bank of Italy. When he gave up the presidency, Giannini's bank salary fell at his insistence to one dollar a year, the figure at which it remained until his death. In this spirit he accepted no further payment, except for the refund of personal and business expenses; he also refused a salary from Bancitaly (later Transamerica) after assuming the presidency of the holding company he had founded, knowing very well that, given its high profits, he could have become a very rich man. Moreover, Giannini spent much of his money for the benefit of his companies and when the commission arrangement came to an end he was no millionaire.[90]

Chapter Nine

FULFILLING DREAMS

When Bancitaly's directors voted, without A.P. knowing, to compensate him with 5% of the corporation's net profits, corresponding to $1.5 million, he insisted that the whole amount be donated right away to the University of California–Berkeley, for the creation of a school of agricultural research and the Giannini Foundation of Agricultural Economics, which supports to this day the world's foremost agricultural economics library and funds cutting-edge research in agriculture, water, and forestry.[91] This major gift from a former fruit peddler was reportedly the country's first philanthropic endowment in the field, with the purpose of raising the profile of agriculture in California. The reaction of the press was extremely positive and incidentally produced favorable publicity, underlining how Giannini was putting his personal wealth at the disposal of university students by encouraging research: "Giannini strips himself of the title of millionaire ... Thus the product of his financial genius has been dedicated to helping all Californians."[92] In this perspective, his bank too continued to personify democracy at work, contributing significantly to the growth and enhancement of his beloved native state and of the West.

With the same spirit, years before, he was the first to unreservedly respond in a concrete way to the bold proposal of a young Italian instructor, Maria Teresa Tommasini Piccirillo, to found a Chair of Italian Culture at the same university. She had arrived from the Italian region of Abruzzi with no English and she graduated with honors from UC Berkeley with a dissertation on D'Annunzio and the French critics. She was asked to teach Italian and immediately realized that there was no specific department of Italian, while the departments of French, Spanish, Chinese, and Japanese were steadily growing. She started contacting businessmen and bankers, getting the most influential members of the Italian colony of San Francisco to share her vision. Giannini's gift of $5,000 toward the Chair was presented in September 1921, initiating a fund-raising campaign, which in less than five years reached her goal of $150,000. The Chair is the only foundation of its kind in the United States and stands as an enduring monument that the Italian-Americans have raised at the University of California, one of the greatest institutions of higher learning.[93]

The fund continues to allow the most qualified Italian scholars from Italy to teach at Berkeley for one academic year, covering varied disciplines such as Literature and Linguistics to Art History and Architecture.[94] Giannini believed in the power of education even though he quit school when he was fifteen, because, after the death of his father, he had more urgent practical tasks to attend to. He helped his brother Attilio and other close friends financially to get their university education. He himself was bilingual and eager to promote the language and culture of his parents and ancestors at an academic level. Very important guests were invited, such as writer and filmmaker Mario Soldati, composers Luigi Dallapiccola and Luciano Berio, architect Ernesto Rogers and writer Giorgio Bassani who were considered part of the Olympus of Italian creativity.

Furthermore, thanks to Mrs. Piccirillo and her tireless energy, the enrollment of students taking Italian at that time became the largest at any university or college in the United States. She used to proudly report in detail her first meeting with A.P. when she candidly told him she needed $150,000 (which corresponds today to about $1.5 million) for the Chair of Italian Culture she envisioned. He amiably asked: "Is it a gold chair?" showing how approachable and gregarious he was. In spite of his jovial reply, he showed great respect for her aspirations and promptly assisted her with the first substantial check. He was a born doer who selflessly helped to turn other people's dreams into reality.

Among A.P.'s most imaginative financing in the period between the two World Wars was in the motion picture industry. Films spoke the universal language of visual images and in the process created a common experience that drew together all the disparate communities then crowding into the New World. The plots of the films were very simple and spoke directly to the aspirations of the hopeful immigrants as well as native-born Americans, fascinated as they were by the dreamlike illusions conjured up in the dark by a roll of celluloid.[95]

Giannini gradually embraced the idea of investing in a medium like the movies, which fully exemplified the idea of democratic participation. At that time, pictures were a popular novelty but hardly anybody was ready to invest in them because, in the existing conditions, they seemed to stand no chance of succeeding.

A.P. and Attilio Giannini were the first bankers to recognize the motion picture business as a legitimate industry. Although A.P. did not always appreciate his brother, he did trust him.

As relative newcomers to the competitive and exclusive world of banking, they chose to collaborate closely. Their different strengths—A.P.'s uncompromising business sense and Attilio's easy grace in social circles—complemented each other. The extent of the affinity between the Gianninis and the pioneers of the movie colony was also extraordinary. It was easy to see why they were able to form such a deep-rooted and enduring alliance.

Just like the film people, the Gianninis were outsiders, immigrants based in the far West, initially distrusted and misunderstood by the financial establishment.[96] A.P.'s "evangelical drive" to open up banking by establishing hundreds of handy informal branches throughout the country, creating a financial system for the masses, was paralleled by the way the movie pioneers brought an increasingly sophisticated entertainment to an audience long excluded from any form of culture.

The Giannini brothers made their first modest loan in the picture industry in 1909 to Sol L. Lesser, a seventeen-year-old partner in a nickelodeon on Fillmore Street in San Francisco, who needed to pay for the delivery of a rented film. By then a kind of "nickel delirium" had swept the country. There were between four and five thousand nickelodeons located across the country offering a dozen or more shows a day. The members of this audience were, almost without exception, poor immigrants new to the city, who could not afford the admission prices or overcome the language barriers of the more conventional forms of entertainment in theaters or vaudeville houses.

So even though young Lesser was told right away that the Bank of Italy did not lend money to finance motion pictures, A.P. decided to advance the money from his personal account because the boy was underage and a dreamer and the bank had no legal means to guarantee repayment. Interestingly enough, Sol

Lesser repaid the loan and later became one of the most successful film exhibitors on the West Coast, passing on the news of the bank's willingness to lend money to some of his colleagues who soon went on to become moguls in the industry.

The nickelodeons marked a real turning point because they provided an affordable entertainment of their own, located—unlike the traditional downtown theaters—in converted stores just a few yards from home. No one was excluded on grounds of origin or education. A new audience was being gradually created on a scale that would have been unimaginable for any established form of entertainment.

A.P was a passionate egalitarian who saw universal access to the arts as the essence of democracy. For him, the little man who paid twenty-five cents for a gallery seat at the cinema deserved the same respect as the rich sophisticated gentleman sitting in his box at the Opera House. Over the next few years he became a fervent supporter of the movie industry, never forgetting how risky that was. However, some risks paid off surprisingly well.

In 1920, he arranged a production loan of $200,000 for self-made movie mogul Cecil B. DeMille to complete *The Ten Commandments*, which won a prestigious Academy Award. Two years later, Giannini made him President of the Bank of Italy's Culver City branch. One of DeMille's first innovations was to reduce the interest on loans from 8% to 7%, thereby attracting many major Hollywood studios. A.P. was very open to initiatives like this, and with DeMille's help also included in the advisory board several influential producers from Hollywood and the chief of MGM.

In 1921, the Bank of Italy loaned $250,000 to First National Distributors to finance the film *The Kid* starring Charlie Chaplin and Jackie Coogan; the loan was repaid in full six weeks after the movie opened. The film was a box-office hit in 1922 and 1923. It cost $500,000 to make and grossed around $2.5 million.

Years later, Chaplin expressed his gratitude by praising A.P. in his autobiography.[97]

Attilio moved to New York in 1919 to manage the East River National at 630 Broadway; the bank was only a few blocks from the theatre and cinema crowd.[98] The Schenck brothers started there before building a studio across the Hudson; others worked as ushers in theatres and movie houses or as waiters, hoping to make a name one day in Hollywood, which some of them did.

Attilio was soon impressed by the early movie-going audience consisting mainly of immigrants and working-class families. Even though in the 1920s the film industry was already in the tenth year of rapid growth, Wall Street bankers were still very reluctant to grant loans to producers. Being a newcomer in New York, Attilio was bold enough "to turn to a business that other bankers did not particularly wish to finance."[99] He became gradually convinced that a film starring Douglas Fairbanks and Charlie Chaplin or any other leading actor was as good as cash, and when he was in doubt he would ask reliable theatre managers for an immediate opinion.

Based on this innovative assumption, if a distributor needed funds to release a picture he would preview the film before an invited audience to test its popular appeal. He also created a system according to which the bank loaned money to fund individual movies and held the film's negative reel as security. Only when the loan had been repaid would the bank authorize the release of the negative from the lab. State banking examiners reacted with dismay to the arrangement of accepting the negative of a completed film as collateral for a loan to begin production on another film. Despite repeated warnings from state bank officials, Bank of Italy continued to believe in this unorthodox form of guarantee.

Giannini included in the board of each bank branch in New York or Los Angeles producers, directors, or leading actors to attract more Hollywood insiders to become depositors or investors. In the end, A.P., and Doc made banking into a branch of show business, scandalizing Wall Street and its conservative representatives such as J. Pierpont Morgan and his peers.[100] They became frequent lenders to the pioneers of the film industry proving that motion picture loans, when properly researched, could offer "security and liquidity."

This is one of the reasons why the movie colony flocked to their bank during the 1920s and 1930s, and for many decades to follow. With Giannini's authorization, Attilio arranged the financing of Columbia Pictures, favoring the industry's growth and its public legitimacy. Attilio was described as "a wop entirely surrounded by Jews and Gentiles"[101] eager to get involved in this new discipline and provide a sympathetic, honest source of credit at the current rate of interest, bypassing greedy money-lenders who could ask rates of interest up to 20%. He simply decided that "motion pictures were good merchandise, as good as cotton, wheat or barley."[102]

Attilio served also as financial adviser to many producers, he settled many conflicts and, being a medical doctor, he assisted some of his clients with gambling and drinking problems. One such client was Jack Warner, head of one of Hollywood's most powerful studios. If on one hand he liked going to parties, always impeccably dressed in a three-piece suit, he was much more than a banker: "everyone in Hollywood cried on his shoulders."[103] Attilio was convinced that through his efforts the bank had achieved a monopoly within the picture business through an extensive network of contacts he created in the industry. Maybe this was an overstatement, but during the 1920s the bank extended more than $100 million in loans to theatre owners and producers.[104]

With three booms going on at once—film industry, oil, and real estate, in addition to the stock market delirium, A.P. was very cautious and refrained from plunging into volatile enterprises and he preferred to follow his own motto: "safety before profit." The collapse of the stock market in 1929 was inevitably followed by a drop in the price of oil, since there was a huge surplus and production had been artificially increased without reference to consumption. Most of Giannini's own troubles were the result of bad investments inherited from purchased banks. Having absorbed the Merchants National of Los Angeles he had a loss in this sector, but a smaller loss than that suffered by J.F. Sartori, who was his main rival in the south.

Giannini was pleased instead to help small homebuyers or store owners, who were less likely to be involved in speculative schemes, unlike large-scale developers. In fact, during the real estate boom, he never granted any loans to builders nor did he sell any trust certificates. He granted almost twice as many real estate loans in San Francisco, an area where there was no boom then as there was in Los Angeles. He felt at ease and willing to help the new incoming minorities who came to California and tried to build a better life for themselves and their families.

He felt particularly attracted to the motion picture industry because it consisted mainly of Jewish producers who were immigrants or from immigrant families, worthy of his consideration and help. He even took a plane to attend the funeral of a young Italian immigrant, Rudolph Valentino, who distinguished himself by becoming a leading silent-film actor. After becoming acquainted with the special needs of this fledgling industry he made his bank the preeminent financier of Hollywood ventures offering honest, average interest rates and never asking for a part of the picture's profit.

Even during the difficult years of the Depression, A.P. took chances with untried ventures, such as in Walt Disney's case. Disney at that time was an unknown animator and dreamer and was considered a rather unorthodox filmmaker who had started from nothing. He had arrived in Hollywood from the Midwest in 1923 with forty dollars and a suitcase full of pens and pencils rather than clothes. A decade later, hundreds of people were employed at his animation factory. A.P. had his first contact with Disney at the very beginning, when he granted him small loans.

A.P. liked Mickey Mouse and provided funds for other shorts such as *Steamboat Willie*, *Silly Symphonies*, and *The Three Little Pigs*.[105] These were very popular short films but only modestly profitable. After a trip to Paris in the 1930s, Disney began considering the possibility of producing a longer film. He saw how the French audiences in packed houses would appreciate several featured cartoons being screened in succession. When he returned to Hollywood he decided to embark on the production of his first feature-length film, based on a Grimm Brothers' fairytale, *Little Snow White*. It was 1931 and Attilio had moved from New York to Los Angeles to become the chairman of Bank of America's regional headquarters in Southern California and was largely responsible for overseeing the accounts there. When Disney asked him for a loan to complete his first full-length cartoon film he was very skeptical because he thought very few people would go and see a film about seven dwarfs.[106]

Disney, however, believed in those dwarfs. He was a perfectionist by nature and was determined to make a top-quality film, but production costs were very high because of the thousands of drawings involved, not to mention the photography and the music. He needed the money to do it right and after Attilio's refusal he was so desperate and out of funds that he decided to go to San Francisco and plead his case directly to A.P. Giannini. A.P. was very impressed by Disney's creativity and relentless determination and decided to reward his passion and his belief in the project by granting him an unprecedented loan of $1.7 million.

Both Giannini and Disney knew that this film was a huge gamble. Had *Snow White* not succeeded, the loss would have bankrupted Disney and hurt the Bank of America badly. The film premiered at New York's Radio City Music Hall on Christmas Day 1937 and was an immediate box-office sensation. It earned more than $22 million in its first nationwide showing.

A.P. was particularly pleased to be able to boast of his courage and good judgment to Attilio. The two brothers were very dissimilar and not entirely appreciative of each other. A.P. considered Attilio vain and ungrateful, while Attilio found his brother authoritarian and crude. Even though Attilio, thanks to his business acumen, was a significant factor in the bank's growth, A.P. was inclined to highlight their differences. After the huge box office hit, A.P. decided to finance Disney's next three full-length animated cartoons: *Dumbo, Fantasia,* and *Pinocchio. Snow White*'s unprecedented success marked a turning point in Disney's business relationship with the Bank of America and in his personal movie-making career, which skyrocketed into a "total merchandising" approach. Helped by A.P., Walt Disney went from rags to riches. When he started, he would have never imagined that his animated films would eventually gross $1 billion a year at the box office and, above all, feed the imaginations of adults and children alike.

Later on, A.P. proved to be capable of fulfilling not only individual dreams but also collective ones, like the building of the Golden Gate Bridge, named in honor of the Golden Horn of the Bosporus that protected the harbor of Constantinople. This was considered by most structural engineers and politicians an impossible endeavor. For years Joseph Strauss, the grandest dreamer of the early 1920s and chief engineer of the project, had proposed a bridge to span the opening of the San Francisco Bay and connect the city to northern California. Of all American regions outside Manhattan, California is the most impressive example of nature rearranged through engineering. From the Gold Rush onward, most Californians lived in cities and suburbs dependent on an elaborate system of water and, later, electrical engineering.[107]

However, designing a suspension bridge that could accommodate great ships and withstand fierce ocean winds, strong currents, and even earthquakes was not an easy task. The enemies of the project were environmentalists because the bridge seemed an arrogant intrusion on nature, and the Southern Pacific Transportation Company objected to the bridge because it threatened the lucrative ferry operations in the San Francisco bay that brought about fifty thousand commuters to the city each day. Government officials doubted the feasibility of the bridge and limited themselves to endorsing and financing only the building of the San Francisco-Oakland Bridge. They showed no interest in backing a second bridge, and Joseph Strauss decided therefore to visit Giannini on August 4, 1932, and had the courage, at the lowest point in the Great Depression, to ask him to consider purchasing the $6 million Golden Gate Bridge District Bonds necessary to begin construction. The meeting took place in Giannini's unpretentious office. Two visionaries were coming into each other's orbit, and the outcome of their conversation would be momentous.[108]

A.P. did some quick calculations in his head; he always knew the numbers that mattered, even though he seldom remembered how much money he had in his own bank account. The bridge was an ambitious and high-profile project, a vehicle for the social and economic development of San Francisco and Northern California, creating immediate jobs and long-term opportunities for the whole region. By agreeing to the plea: "We need the bridge!" he agreed to buy the bonds and recognized the importance of fast and reliable transportation around the Bay for trade and business. If the bridge could be built, San Francisco would benefit and the Bank of America would get recognition of this unprecedented, epic achievement of American labor. On the other hand, if A.P. agreed to purchase bonds for a bridge that could not be built, the bank would look reckless and irresponsible. "How long would this bridge last?" Giannini asked Strauss at the conclusion of their meeting. "Forever," Strauss replied with great prescience.

He believed, from that moment on, that the possible rewards of the bridge would outweigh the considerable risk. Joseph Strauss walked out of the bank with a promise for the money he so desperately needed. Construction of the Golden Gate Bridge began five months later. It proved a masterstroke of finance and public relations. The result was a global icon, a triumph of engineering, and a work of art. The Golden Gate Bridge assured an American generation that the Great Depression could be overcome by a fruitful interaction between public and private investment and between material culture and social purpose, proving once again that Giannini's powerful intuition and forward thinking were always for the benefit of the community at large.[109]

Chapter Ten

NATIONWIDE BANKING: A LIFE-LONG MISSION

Besides his educational and civic aspirations, A.P. still dreamed of a nationwide branch banking system, extending from coast to coast and ultimately globally. Deep down he knew he had to purchase a prestigious bank, a bastion within the Wall Street establishment, as the first step towards making his goal of transcontinental banking a reality.

The banking capital of the nation was three thousand miles away and the most powerful banks in the country had their headquarters there. Never one to think small, A.P. wanted his bank to stand beside them, and now he had the financial power to make it so. Moreover, by the late 1920s there were already eight hundred thousand Italian immigrants living in Manhattan, Brooklyn, and the Bronx, almost twice as many as in the whole of San Francisco.

His desire to conquer Wall Street had already surfaced in 1912 when he traveled to New York with a view to opening a branch with the leaders of the Italian community. He had sent Armando Pedrini to negotiate the deal, which fell through because he was not then ready to leave California to manage the branch as the sellers had requested. In 1919, he bought the East

River National Bank as a first outlet in New York and sent his brother Attilio to direct it. But this was not enough.

To reach his goal, nine years later he sent his agent, Leo Belden, to scout New York's banking scene and finally decided to acquire the Bank of America at 44 Wall Street, one of the city's oldest financial institutions. Founded in 1812, it had a sterling reputation and historically it had absorbed the First United States Bank, which attempted branch banking as far back as 1791.[110] Moreover, it had close connections to the legendary House of Morgan.

Giannini had no idea of the high price he would have to pay to fulfill his lifelong banking dream, which would entail first coming to terms with J.P. Morgan, the New York tycoon. He felt he had to ask for Morgan's consent since he was still the most powerful single financial force in the country, but this proved to be a fatal miscalculation on A.P.'s part. The House of Morgan was at the corner of Wall and Broad and was often referred to as "the Corner." The transaction was concluded in March 1928. Giannini bought a majority of shares in the Bank of America for $17 million and merged it with Bowery East River National Bank and the Commercial Exchange to form the Bank of America National Association.

Suddenly Giannini owned the third-largest bank in New York. This major acquisition was possible thanks mainly to the record profits of Bancitaly. Giannini's three headquarters now were San Francisco, New York, and Los Angeles and according to the *San Francisco Bulletin* of the same year, an invasion of "London, Paris, and Berlin appears to set the stage for entrance of A.P. Giannini as the new colossus of the world finance."[111]

In the few weeks before the old shares in the three component banks could be exchanged for shares in the new Bank of

America, they doubled or tripled in price generating a "speculative orgy," a sort of frenzy that Giannini had in fact anticipated and tried vehemently to curb.[112] *Forbes* magazine had praised Giannini's daring, ability, foresight, and unselfishness. It remarked that A.P. Giannini was ahead of everybody else and pointed out that since there was insufficient profit in straight commercial banking, the winning idea of transforming the bank of tomorrow into a sort of department store was starting an unprecedented financial revolution. The *Wall Street Journal* had also reminded its readers of the California banker's wise advice urging stockholders to limit their purchases only to what they could afford.

Unfortunately, under Morgan's influence, the Federal Reserve Bank of New York soon required A.P. to convert Bancitaly stock to individual ownership and operate as a trust company rather than as a holding operation, as a necessary step to the Bank of America going nationwide.

A.P. reluctantly complied, knowing that from that moment on he would be able to exercise very little control over speculation in the bank's stock.

While A.P was eager to start his own bank, possibly tapping the mass market of millions of small depositors and lenders, Morgan was not willing to let a bold newcomer from California take the lead. The whole New York banking community was very wary of this ex-fruit peddler joining their select ranks. They did not particularly like this Italian immigrant's son, a Catholic, and of California farm provenance.

True to his roots, A.P. wanted small investors to be welcome at all his democratic banks from North Beach to Wall Street and be able to deposit "from one dollar up." The New York establishment instead looked upon small saving accounts with contempt and viewed western banks as risky and unreliable. The New York contingent was exclusively in favor of a market of upper class people of wealth.[113] Morgan at the beginning seemed friendly but soon after he felt he could dictate and impose all kinds of other demands with the clear intention of making Giannini's life difficult. He requested from A.P. an extra deposit of $1 million in a Morgan bank, in addition to what they had already negotiated.

Only then was the consolidation of the three banks agreed upon as well as the addition of NT (National Trust) & SA (Savings Association) to the final title for the conversion into a national bank. Morgan played a dominant role in the selection of the Bank of America NT&SA staff. The Long Island aristocrat Edward Delafield remained President and Attilio Giannini became Chairman of the Board. Morgan also chose the new board of directors, relegating most Italian-Americans to an irrelevant advisory board slot with inadequate office space. Attilio became immediately suspicious and irritated when Delafield tried to deny him the right to preside over at the first general meeting. Moreover, the salaries of the Morgan men were increased soon after and their expense accounts expanded unjustifiably. However, Giannini was so eager to go ahead with his New York plans that he asked Attilio to be patient, at least to begin with.

A new wave of troubles and humiliations lay ahead, given the fact that A.P. and his Italian-American "gang" were perceived as invading what had been until then a Yankee stronghold. Giannini acquired his Eastern bastion in the hope of turning it into the hub of a powerful transcontinental banking system but he knew deep down that he had compromised more than he ever had before. Leo Belden, his agent, was in awe of Morgan and always ready to comply with his growing demands. Besides, his archenemy F. Sartori had sent a letter to twenty-eight thousand bank presidents urging them to start a national movement against Giannini in order to stymie him and his plans.[114]

After he had acquired the Bank of America he felt exhausted and upset by the constant swing of his bank's stocks, and in April he left for Europe for over four months with his wife Clorinda and daughter Claire for a rest, in the hope that this vacation would have a sobering effect on the market. The reverse proved to be true. Rising stock prices followed him from Chicago to Paris to Milan, where he was heralded by a spree on the local exchange in the shares of *Banca d'America e d'Italia* and a new subsidiary called *Ameritalia*. In Rome he had lunch with Benito Mussolini at Palazzo Chigi, the dictator's residence. He had been heralded by the country's leading Fascist newspaper, *Popolo d'Italia,* as "the Napoleon of high finance" as well as "the greatest banker in the world, equal if not greater than Morgan, Rockefeller or Ford." Mussolini had hoped to include Giannini in a campaign among Americans of Italian descent to financially support his government.[115] There is no evidence, however, as to whether Giannini cooperated or not with his endeavors. What we do know, as Giannini himself admitted, is that Mussolini benefited directly during the 1920s from his successful transactions in Europe.

In Italy, Giannini also encountered Count Volpi di Misurata. He was a prominent Italian financier whose industrial reputation was worldwide. As finance minister he had successfully negotiated Italy's World War I debt repayment with the United States and with England, and pegged the value of the lira to the value of gold. Giannini in those days was also considering aiding Italian industries with a substantial amount of money. When word of a proposed new auxiliary corporation to be founded in

Italy was leaked, thousands of inexperienced investors plunged into an unwarranted purchase of the stock at high prices. In spite of the fact that A.P had ordered the Bank of Italy and all its branches to stop selling the Italian stock, the American press was hailing a second California Gold Rush and the profits it had generated for the many common people who had bought Giannini's shares. Hundreds of humble investors had become affluent, thanks to the Italian-American wizard of finance. When Blue Monday struck on June 11, 1928, the stocks of Bancitaly, Bank of Italy, and Bank of America lost from 30.3% to 43.8%. Speculators who used them as collateral for additional purchases of the same stock without having the money to pay for them, ran up losses of millions of dollars and many people were forced to sell their fine houses and change their lifestyles.

While A.P. lay ill in bed with polyneuritis at the Excelsior Hotel in Rome, surrounded by specialists, the Bank of America stock plunged even further. The painful and debilitating inflammation of the nerves and muscles plagued him for several months. Giannini, unable to eat or sleep, barely able to walk, was taken for treatment to a specialist on Lake Nemi, forty miles outside of Rome. He had done everything in his power to curb speculations; he had even given precise instructions to withhold credit from people trying to promote unhealthy financial gambling and for a while secretly decided, along with his son Mario, also sick at the Saint Francis Hospital in San Francisco, to support the stocks with insider buying for $60 million.

In spite of these strenuous and heroic efforts to try to protect the stockholders, there seemed to be a well-coordinated movement against Giannini's stock. By mid-June, after over a week of constant decline, prices stabilized and began to slowly climb again. In the meantime, Bancitaly's capital had suffered a combined loss of approximately $20 million due to this major financial maelstrom.[116]

A.P. was particularly disappointed with Bacigalupi's unexpected indecision and weakness in handling the crisis. The market had been manipulated thanks possibly to the joint efforts of Giannini's major competitor and vice president of the Anglo-California Bank, Herbert Fleishhacker, joining forces with J.P. Morgan and other Wall Street opportunists, including Leo Belden, Giannini's chief emissary to New York's financial community. Belden, he suspected, might easily have been one of the co-conspirators who successfully pushed down his stock in order to discredit Giannini's financial institutions. He had obviously sold out to J.P. Morgan for personal gain.

In spite of the fact that Belden continued to deny every accusation, the most striking evidence of his guilt emerged later on, from a report that made public Morgan's preferred list of clients to whom the firm sold stock at a price far below prevailing market standards. The name of Leo Belden was included, proving once more that Giannini's unfailing intuition had been correct.

Giannini's own reputation was on the line so he decided to return to the States as soon as he could, and ask Louis Ferrari, Bank of Italy's trust attorney and chief legal counsel, to propose an investigation by the Department of Justice into the unprecedented bear raid. He also wanted to found a sort of parent corporation embracing a large family of branch banks with the precise goal of curbing dangerous market fluctuations. He was quite convinced that this conspiracy was a violation of common law.

On August 22, he managed to embark on the *Ile de France* in Paris, bound for New York, the first leg of his return trip home. When the ship docked, reporters commented that his appearance was "showing the results of his long and terrible suffering." In particular the correspondent of *The New York Times* noted that he looked emaciated and walked with difficulty, but was able to comment on the Blue Monday crash although prudently sticking to a carefully worded statement prepared by Bacigalupi, fearing that he would denounce J.P. Morgan and Company for a cleverly concocted conspiracy. Instead, he said that he had predicted the bear raid and so had warned against speculation but had been ignored; he also praised at length his executives for handling the crisis "with flying colours."[117] The next morning, along with Bacigalupi and Hale, Giannini reluctantly met Francis Bartow, a junior partner in J.P. Morgan and Co. at the Bank of America headquarters, for a brief encounter in which Giannini was bitterly reproached for having supported the market during the dramatic month of June, sacrificing an outstanding amount of money for personal ambition.

Giannini was bluntly reminded that he was given a rare opportunity to establish his bank in New York but on the implied condition that he would play the Wall Street game. Claiming ill health, Giannini postponed their next meeting by a few weeks.

He felt betrayed, sad, and vulnerable. He was a gentle and jovial giant of great moral integrity. He knew his personal *via crucis* had started due to unforeseen humiliation and physical pain. He also knew that the only remedies to all these new trials were courage, vision, and willpower in the pursuit of a worthwhile goal.

Once back in San Francisco, he was so delighted to be greeted by his son Mario who had himself recovered from an illness although he was still walking with a cane. When he saw hundreds of old multilingual friends waiting for him at the bank on Powell Street, and his desk covered in flowers, he immediately felt better and "fit to be back in the saddle."[118] His plan of founding the greatest holding company ever was quickly taking shape, but he purposely did not keep "the Corner" informed of his moves. The name *Transamerica* was suggested by Rose Walter, Louis Ferrari's secretary. It conveyed exactly what Giannini had in mind, a giant umbrella holding company and a repository for the stocks of his banks that he hoped would become available from ocean to ocean.[119] Such an endeavor required a great deal of corporate procedure because Bancitaly, Bank of Italy, Bank of America, and a host of various affiliated institutions had all to become subsidiaries of Transamerica Corporation on January 1, 1929.

Both A.P. and Mario made sure that the company had a majority of Californians on the board to recover full control of the situation, since the loyalty and confidence of these stockholders never faded. The stock of the Bank of Italy and the Bancitaly Corporation were removed from the various exchanges and only the new Transamerica Corporation stock was then admitted to the San Francisco and New York Stock Exchange. The deposits that year increased while Bancitaly was dissolved. The founding of Transamerica, however, worsened the tension between A.P. and Wall Street. He bravely withdrew all the accounts of the Bank of Italy and the Bank of America from J.P. Morgan & Co. Without any hesitation, Transamerica acquired 63% of the outstanding shares of the Bank of America NT&SA. He was ready to continue his New York financial activity without Morgan's approval after being arbitrarily discredited because he knew that Morgan was doing everything possible, directly or indirectly, to force his bank out of Wall Street or at least to stunt its growth.[120]

As an Italian-American, in 1929 Giannini got great satisfaction from being awarded a Knighthood of the Order of Malta, the oldest and most distinguished honor granted by the Vatican. The same year the King of Italy Vittorio Emanuele III awarded him a gold medal for having established and maintained the Chair of Italian Culture at the University of California–Berkeley. Shortly afterwards he also saw his application finally accepted by the Pacific Union Club, the most influential gathering place for businessmen and politicians in San Francisco.

It was on October 17, 1929, that A.P. hosted two dinner parties, one at the Fairmont Hotel with more than a thousand employees in attendance, to celebrate the twenty-fifth anniversary of the one-room bank he had opened less than a mile away; and a more intimate one at the club in honor of Bacigalupi, who had become the vice chairman of the advisory committee of the Transamerica Corporation. Giannini strongly believed in the practice of rotating his top executives every five years because he was convinced that "when a man has a chance to go up the ladder instead of having to wait for the chief to die, it stimulates him to concentrate on his job and to achieve something."[121] Moreover, A.P. himself finally felt recognized in his hometown and the club provided him with the respect he deserved, after ignoring him for too many years. Soon his bank would be open to more than just Italians or Californians.

Chapter Eleven

BETRAYAL FROM WITHIN

After twenty-six years of exceptional service and a kaleido-scopic life, A.P. intended to change the bank's name from Bank of Italy to Bank of America National Trust and Savings Association, serving all Americans.

In spite of the doctors' recommendations to work less, Giannini invested a lot of his physical and intellectual energies in the growth of branch banking globally. In the spring of 1929, he absorbed Blair and Company, one of the foremost private banking firms in America with activities of international scope. They financed important railroads and granted loans to foreign governments. From what he knew of their work, he admired Elisha P. Walker, the president of Blair and some of his energetic executives, including the brilliant Jean Monnet, a highly regard-ed French industrial expert and former deputy secretary of the League of Nations. He knew that in a few years his son Mario would be seasoned enough to lead his financial empire. At thir-ty-five, Mario was already one of the country's most respected bankers. In the meantime, A.P. was looking for a Wall Street man with the financial ability to be able to run his mega-cor-poration and succeed him. Walker was almost fifty years old, a native New Yorker and a graduate of Yale and the Massachusetts Institute of Technology. He seemed to have all the ingredients of a leader, capable of fighting off raids on his stocks, and the human qualities to make him a worthy president of an institution that had been run for twenty-five years exclusively in a spirit of service.

Thinking he had found the right successor, Giannini prepared Transamerica for great changes. Blair and Company became the investment arm of the Bank of America and Walker was appointed President of the firm and Chairman of the Bank of America Executive Committee.

Walker made several long visits to California in late 1929 to get acquainted with his new duties and responsibilities. He spent the historic day of October 24, 1929, with A.P. This marked the beginning of the most titanic financial crash ever witnessed in American history. In the attempt to defend the value of Transamerica stock, Giannini supported the market by buying all of the 230,000 shares of Transamerica that had been dumped on the San Francisco Stock Exchange. It was a hasty and rather reckless action, which unfortunately did not serve its purpose. Blue Monday in 1928 had been just a warning, targeted mainly at Giannini's stocks, and the March 1929 jolt a sharper reminder, so the Federal Reserve Board issued strong warnings against further speculation.

It was impossible to withstand the bear market of October 1929. Giannini did what he could, spending hours trying to peg Transamerica at $60 but it was not enough. It inevitably fell to $32. The same was true for the House of Morgan, which tried to make up a pool to support the market but to no effect.

On the so-called "Black Tuesday" in October 1929, the market collapsed and panic took over. It was the end of an era. After seven years of great profits and sound investments, the 1929 crash overturned all securities, causing "a bitter downward spiral of economic activity affecting every phase and aspect of human life."[122] Everything in the United States was shaken to the foundation, including Wall Street. This ushered in the Depression, an unprecedented ten-year period of economic hardship and unemployment, which put on hold every dream of further expansion. In 1930, many workers lost their jobs and homes; unemployment increased by an average of 750,000 people a month; over 1,300 banks failed (only eight of which were in California) and many people risked losing their hard-earned savings.

Giannini seemed paradoxically unaffected by this devastating stock market crash, which he called "a market slump," a real understatement. He firmly believed the American people had to face the future with optimism and therefore decided to finance the completion of the Hetch Hetchy Aqueduct, San Francisco's water and power supply system, with a substantial $41 million bond. The press praised this as "an act of patriotism and loyalty to the people of San Francisco."[123] Giannini did not intend to change his plan, totally engaged as he was in establishing his mega-transcontinental corporation as well as getting ready to turn it over to a younger leader. His sixtieth birthday was approaching and he wanted to be "on the sidelines again, this time for good."

In January 1930, Walker, with less than a year's experience in the Giannini organization, retired from the presidency of Bancamerica-Blair, became Chairman of the Board of Directors and chief executive officer of Transamerica with a yearly salary of $100,000. Jean Monnet was made vice chairman with a salary of $50,000 and Mario Giannini, next to Walker in importance, became president with a salary also of $50,000. A.P. had chosen him as his eventual successor further down the line, and rightly so, since Mario was a talented banker, appreciated also for his unusual humility and respect for his father. Throughout his life he always tried hard to prove himself worthy of A.P.'s trust and expectations. A.P. was pleased to accept only the nominal chairmanship of the Advisory Committee of the new Transamerica.

The press recognized right away that A.P., though off the payroll, was the brain and the power behind the throne and that Transamerica was becoming the nation's preeminent financial institution. As the *San Francisco Examiner* reported: "There is probably no banker in the country today who is in the advantageous position in which Giannini finds himself. The prospects for the future are startling. It seems extremely probable that future developments affecting Transamerica will attract public interest sooner or later, as great, or even greater, than anything we have ever seen before."[124]

The contract with Walker was signed on January 16, 1930, and consisted of two complementary sections: the first was about the firm commitment of pursuing nationwide branch banking and the second highlighted the importance of the Bank of America, which was to become one of the leading financial institutions in New York.

Each time Elisha Walker went to San Francisco to acquaint himself with his new associates, the *San Francisco Chronicle* reported with great enthusiasm the arrival of the new chairman of Transamerica, stressing his complete adherence to the guidelines of the founder A.P. Giannini. Walker would strongly reiterate that Transamerica would continue to be an institution run solely in the interest of the stockholders and of the depositors and that he personally would be totally devoted to pursuing a nationwide branch banking policy, as well as large liquid reserves and sound investments. All this was also specified and co-signed in a personal agreement of understanding with A.P., with a view to keeping Transamerica growing nationwide and internationally.

To direct his New York headquarters, Giannini had surprised everyone by appointing an experienced Wall Street banker, but he was someone completely outside his own milieu. A.P.'s faulty judgment in selecting his successor ended up creating unforeseen difficulties. After turning sixty on May 6, he wanted to take greater care of his health; he seemed at peace with himself and content to let someone else competently oversee his banking empire.

A.P. considered Transamerica's future very promising, in spite of the crucially difficult time for the national economy. The corporation had weathered the market crash without major losses. A.P. was leaving Transamerica with resources totaling about $3 billion. It owned stock in every leading bank in the United States and Canada. It also held huge interests in many European banks, including Italy, where it owned a number of banks from Milan to Naples. He felt he had chosen his leaders wisely. He was leaving behind him a board of directors consisting mainly of old friends and faithful associates who had built their careers on the basis of respect and competence. All of this was the creation of one man's dream and the key to it was branch banking. It was what the world needed. It would allow the present banks to establish themselves in any part of the world with lower operating costs and fewer losses. It would provide "safer and more adequate banking services because of a greater diversification of assets, a greater capital investment, and a greater credit capacity," as Giannini often insisted.

Mario, the corporation's new president, was sincerely impressed by the new chairman's ambitious goals and confidence, and also thought the prospects for the future were bright; he felt proud of being part of such a great institution and honored with the responsibility handed down to him by his father.

Attilio by contrast was much more skeptical. He wrote to Pedrini about what he feared was sure to happen: "What A.P. built up seems to have been emasculated overnight." The reason for this dramatic conviction was that Attilio understood very well that the Wall Street bankers, in particular Morgan, cared only for their own financial interests and could not be trusted. He was therefore very unhappy over his brother's decision to have appointed Walker and Monnet as the corporation's chief executive officers.

Before long, Giannini himself started to be deeply worried and unsatisfied, if not anguished, with their leadership, which soon proved weak and ineffective. He received a great number of complaints from investors about Walker's silence on any of the stocks' earnings as well on the record earnings of Transamerica, which had been increased at the end of 1929 by over $96 million, as noted by the *San Francisco Chronicle*.[125] Delafield's malicious new policy at the New York headquarters of the Bank of America, selling stocks at lower prices, immediately alerted and upset Attilio. He was convinced that there was a "sinister purpose" behind this unnecessary policy and that the Wall Street gang was trying to "throw them out of the picture" by creating a chain reaction of panic leading to a possible bear raid. He warned Mario in writing: "If you wish to retain control you had better get someone on the job quick. You had better come here and tell these fellows where they head in or else what your dad built up all these years will very soon go completely into strangers' hands. I do not want to wait for that evil day."[126] Walker and the Gianninis had very different ideas, outlook, and training, and the whole economic world was falling apart because of the Depression.

A.P., however, had planned a trip to Europe with his wife and daughter and was too exhausted to start another fierce battle right away. Since his return from Rome almost two years earlier, he had been under severe pressure and in constant pain because of his worsening polyneuritis and pleurisy. The doctors had recommended absolute rest if he did not want to become crippled or even die. Six months after releasing his formal retirement statement, A.P. left for Europe, with the clear intention of being in constant touch with his son Mario. By visiting some European spas, renowned for their hot sulfur baths and mineral waters, he was hoping to find some relief. While A.P. was crossing the Atlantic, Transamerica stocks plunged from $45 to $37.75 in two days. The *Los Angeles Times* immediately reported "a well-organized bear raid emanating from the east coast" while the financial editor of the *San Francisco Chronicle* was even more outspoken in his report. He quickly connected the new Transamerica's acquisition of the First National Bank, Portland, to the alleged raid and wrote a devastating piece: "Those persons in the east, desiring to embarrass the Giannini organization in its expansion program, obviously could attempt to do it in no better way than through a raid on the stocks."[127]

Now that Giannini was out and the Depression was raging on, rumors started circulating that Transamerica was one of the weakest stocks on the market. During his first overseas stop in London, A.P. read a disconcerting article in the *London Daily Mail* underlining the difference of $30 million between the figures indicated by Walker as Transamerica earnings in 1929 and the ones indicated by him before leaving. Instead of answering A.P.'s telegram with a convincing explanation of the embarrassing discrepancy, Walker showed concern only for the public image of the bank and invited him to avoid any discussion of this kind in the press. When Giannini informed Bacigalupi he intended to cancel his trip to Karlsbad and face Walker in person on the matter, Bacigalupi with the help of Pedrini and Hale urged him to give Walker more time because his sudden return would have thrown the stockholders into a selling panic, causing further damage. Giannini very reluctantly agreed to carry on to his destination but every day became more and more inclined to believe that he had become a victim of a coast-to-coast sabotage. Once he was in Karlsbad, a health resort in Czechoslovakia, polyneuritis hit him again very severely. He felt as if a million knives were piercing his nerves. It was a dramatic warning of the imminent betrayal to come.

Walker, Monnet, and Delafield had calculated deliberately and astutely every move in setting up their lethal trap. They now began to execute their plan. Giannini found out from Mario in the meantime that Belden, who had been fired three months earlier, had opened a brokerage business in San Francisco and had become the closest ally of Herbert Fleishhacker, president of the Anglo California Bank, Giannini's competitor since Jimmy Rolph's mayoral campaign in the fall of 1927, and his archenemy. Their intent was to drive down the price of Transamerica stocks for a second time, repeating the dirty New York trick of "Blue Monday." Mario had hired a team of private detectives, following his father's example, and had received clear proof of treachery and well-orchestrated intrigue.

Walker and Monnet had decided to definitely eliminate the bank's dividend and cut expenses. Mario sensed more and more the threat to Transamerica and became sure of their hidden "new intentions" to the point that he wired his suspicions to his pain-ridden father. He was sure by now that Walker was determined to gradually dismember the Bank of America from within, by paring it down. By now, both A.P. and Mario knew that they were surrounded by conspirators.

Certain that the survival of Transamerica was at stake, Giannini decided that the only option left was to return to San Francisco and reassume control. Moreover, on August 8, 1930, the Transamerica stocks plunged to $18. While Walker was ready to transform Transamerica the way he had planned, Giannini, despite his condition, was getting physically and spiritually stronger and morally confident enough to resume his old duties, repair the damage done by choosing the wrong successor, and fight back against the gang once and for all.

On August 17, 1930, Giannini left for San Francisco after he received a cablegram that his adored stepfather Lorenzo Scatena, Chairman of the Board of the Bank of Italy, was very sick and doctors did not expect him to survive. He arrived in six days, a record for those times, but it was not enough. When he reached his stepfather's house in Sausalito, his father had already died. He was buried next to his wife at the Holy Cross Cemetery. He had proven to be a truly caring father to the three children of the widow he married. For the first time since the death of his father Luigi when he was only a child, Giannini cried, as Claire remembered in a private interview.[128]

After overcoming his personal grief and deep feeling of loss, he went back to business. At this stage he was hoping to get Walker and Monnet quietly out of the organization, with the help of his old lieutenants. Nobody knew then that for several months they had secretly been meeting Thomas Lamont, senior partner in the firm of J.P. Morgan. The scope of Morgan's involvement in the sudden Transamerica financial decline was by then not a proven fact but there was a strong suspicion on Giannini's part, who accused Walker and Monnet of duplicity. He tried to convince his closest Bank of Italy associates to remove them, but Bacigalupi, Pedrini, and Hale were not in favor of further reorganization and insisted instead on Giannini's cooperation in reassuring the old stockholders since morale was quite low after the further decline of the stock market. At a series of meetings several key changes were made, including the merger of the Bank of Italy and Bank of America California under the title of Bank of America National Trust and Savings Association on September 3, 1930. After twenty-six years of relentless activity, no other private bank had fought more winning battles than the Bank of Italy, which was now coming quietly to its end.

The Bank of America NT&SA had the same directors and officers both as a federal and state institution. As chairman of the committee Giannini minutely laid out all the details of the consolidation. Their combined worth was about a billion and a quarter dollars and the press reacted very positively, underlining how this decision marked a step forward in Giannini's ambitious goal of establishing a coast-to-coast network of branch banks. A.P. was convinced by Bacigalupi to be patient and participate in a ten-day swing across the state to discuss this important announcement with the stockholders; but in reality the intent was to introduce them to the new chief executive officers, Walker and Monnet.

Giannini felt strongly that they were both brilliant actors rather than convinced supporters of his corporation. Giannini's presence was highly welcomed and applauded by overflowing crowds in attendance from Sacramento to San Diego. The tour was concluded with a surge of optimism in Los Angeles at the Biltmore Hotel where Walker spoke with great confidence and trust in the Transamerica stock, reassuring the audience that he would never sell his securities and that he was about to rapidly establish branch banking in every single state and abroad. But in the fall a new economic crisis followed, unemployment was the highest in the nation's history, the profits of leading American industries had fallen from 45 to 60% and Transamerica stock plunged again from 14 to 11, despite the operations of a supporting pool.

Time magazine dedicated a long article to maintaining that the shares had been unnecessarily devaluated and that Amadeo Peter Giannini, while ill in Miami, had denounced illegal manipulations of the nation's securities and urged the stockholders to build a "united front against the enemy," meaning the speculators or leaders of a bear movement as well as one specific competitor, in particular, whose name was intentionally not specified. The reference was clearly to the prominent San Francisco banker Herbert Fleishhacker. At the same time Giannini had called for a Congressional investigation, given the frequency of these gambling operations and the huge financial losses they were inflicting on Transamerica stockholders. For the first time Giannini made his suspicions public, which irritated Walker no end because these allegations appeared in the most important American dailies from the *New York Times* to the *San Francisco Chronicle*. Walker instead never made an issue of bear operations and actually went to offer Fleishhacker his apologies in person.

Giannini was sure by now that Walker and Monnet were acting in the interests of Wall Street and were involved in a "diabolical conspiracy with market bears like Fleishhacker and Belden to drive small shareholders out of the corporation, seizing complete control of Transamerica and silencing, once and for all, the voice of California and its management."[129]

According to the annual statement, Transamerica's profits plunged at the end of 1930 to $18,537,000 against the $67,316,000 of 1929 when Walker joined the corporation.[130]

Mario Giannini and Elisha Walker were very different from each other, in fact, they were poles apart. Their relationship started deteriorating a month after the Bank of Italy changed its name. In the fall and winter of 1930, decisions were gradually made only in New York; Mario was never consulted on important issues, but was informed indirectly through third parties, and reduced to a chronic objector to policies he had never shaped. Mario's resignation was at that point inevitable. Meanwhile, A.P. and his family had made plans in early 1931 for a continental journey, with hopes of it being a "pleasure trip only." He left Miami for Bad Gastein, a health resort in the Austrian Alps, trying to regain his strength, as he wrote to Pedrini on Christmas Day: "Oh, how I do wish, Ped, I could have my old health back again for a while, say just a year or so, and be there constantly on the firing line with you all and properly showing Herbert Fleishhacker et al."[131] In Austria, however, the old scourge struck again, more agonizing than ever. In the meantime, an emergency meeting had taken place in New York where a drastic program of contraction and restructuring was decided along with Bacigalupi, entailing "a liquidation of certain corporate assets."

Mario, who had not been invited to attend, decided to resign after he had scheduled a private clarifying meeting with Walker, which was denied. He had previously been kept waiting outside Walker's office on more than one occasion. He had had enough of being looked upon with contempt and being treated with no respect in his role as president.

In the beginning A.P. was incredulous and made a number of exorbitantly expensive trans-Atlantic calls to Walker in New

York and Bacigalupi in San Francisco, which were never refunded. Before stepping down from Transamerica, a sum had been set aside as a retirement fund for him, instead of a previously voted compensation, which was then denied "by the present board of directors." Giannini tried for a while to keep an honest, open relationship with his friend Bacigalupi, as in the old times, commenting on Walker's brazen proposals, but soon realized that he too had changed sides and was now part of the New York conspiracy. In a bitter and heartfelt cable he declared to him: "I am not the man to stand by and see my *model child* put to death" and even more directly: "Lawton—code name for Walker—will find in me one stockholder who can't be bought off. No sir, Jim, never!" He was convinced more than ever that stockholders were the only ones entitled to decide whether Walker's new destructive policy had to be adopted or challenged. Walker wasted no time in appointing Bacigalupi as Transamerica's new president.

Soon after, A.P. himself reached the irrevocable decision to resign as well, following Mario's example. An article in *Time* underlined right away how three decades of Giannini's control had suddenly come to an end.[132] Attilio too was on the point of resigning because of the opposite motivations driving the new management but decided to postpone his decision for a little while. We will see later how A.P. managed to regain total control of the situation in southern California thanks to the fact that Attilio soon after was transferred by Walker to Los Angeles, thinking he would be out of the way there. Instead, he would play a major role in his brother's triumphant resurgence.

At the end of February, the federal bank examiners had noticed, in a confidential report, that the total of loans of Transamerica had dramatically decreased and that doubtful loans had surprisingly increased from $3,000,000 to $11,000,000. During the first six months of 1931, the Bank of America NT&SA had a loss in deposits of 8.8% while the state bank had a loss of 5.7%. The bank still made a profit but in order to keep afloat, the staff was cut by 10%, which meant that 850 people were laid off.[133]

On June 17, 1931, Walker's drastic reorganization plans were totally endorsed by an overzealous Bacigalupi, in view of a severe debt of $51,800,000 the corporation had to face. On top of that he had been pressured by the Comptroller of the Currency to pay $15,000,000 to cover bank loans, marked off as losses. Bacigalupi, Pedrini, and the old Bank of Italy pals had clearly traded their loyalty to Walker for their own self-interest and became co-conspirators and therefore approved a new program of contraction and liquidation to be carried out by cutting dividends, selling Transamerica's interest in Bank of America N.A. (New York), and eventually S.A. (California). In other words, according to Giannini, they intended "to knock down value and, after this value has been publicly established, go out and sell."[134] All of this was approved "in principle" by the board, and ironically enough, "in the best interest of Transamerica and its stockholders."

Giannini, still in terrible pain, went on to Berlin from Bad Gastein to see more specialists for his persistent polyneuritis, to get himself in shape to fight back and "give those dirty crooks a battle when the right moment to strike arrives." Despite his personal trouble and the biggest financial recession ever, A.P. kept his fighting spirit alive. He was outraged that someone he had personally appointed was trying from within to dismantle an economic empire that it had taken him "twenty-seven years of hard work" to build. The morale of the stockholders and employees further deteriorated when it became evident that the Merchants National Bank in Los Angeles had been mismanaged and large sums had been withdrawn by top officers for personal use.

In the meantime, the liquidation of more "corporate assets" was decided at yet another meeting of the Board of Directors as well as at a special stockholders' reunion meeting that was called for July 21, 1931, and approved by less than half of the total bank executives. It was a complete victory for Walker. Interestingly enough, Giannini's suggestion to establish a committee, independent of the management, to study the issue and submit it to the stockholders was not even considered. Moreover, his resignation was deliberately announced only in September and with misleading unofficial innuendos. Walker had started a vicious campaign with the intent of discrediting Giannini personally, raising doubts concerning his previous salary and his personal fortune. A.P. valued his integrity too much to let these malicious rumors circulate uncontested and was eager to inform the public accordingly.

The board of directors now included Walker associates from Wall Street as well as James Bacigalupi as the new president, who had become more manipulative than ever, and other long-time Bank of Italy employees, including Armando Pedrini, who had been, according to Giannini, "bought off through social attentions, tips, salaries" and threatened with being fired if he did not toe the top management's line.

Walker started to prepare a comprehensive communication to be sent to the stockholders informing them about his new plans. When Giannini found out that things were moving quickly, he decided to take action right away. Mario booked a trans-Atlantic crossing to Canada under the name of S.A. Williams, without informing anyone. On September 4, 1931, A.P. reached Quebec and took a train to meet Mario in Vancouver. They boarded a ferry to Seattle and then drove five hundred miles south to Lake Tahoe, a mountain resort in California, which they thought was the perfect place to discuss their strategy for coping with the conspiracy and hopefully defeating their enemies. They knew they had been deprived of any support, since the whole board had succumbed to the intimidating authority of Wall Street and therefore they had to conduct the fight on their own, trying to re-establish "an institution with soul," working only in the interest of the stockholders, and therefore counting entirely on the latter's endorsement.[135]

This was the only way to defy the Wall Street school of finance aimed at knocking down the value of every component and selling out Transamerica, his lifetime endeavor. They started discussing the involvement of his old archenemy Herbert Fleishhacker and Leo Belden in selling Transamerica's shares below value and were considering starting a legal action against Walker and Monnet on charges of fraud. Two days after his arrival there, A.P. left his cabin to go to the barber's for a haircut and shave when he found himself face to face with the last person on earth he wanted to see: Fleishhacker, who was vacationing there with his family. That same day the San Francisco press announced Giannini's return to California. Before leaving Lake Tahoe for San Mateo, Giannini sent Bacigalupi a defiant telegram announcing war on Walker and Monnet. He was sure that both men were in agreement with his enemies on Wall Street aiming to seize full control of the corporation in a conspiracy to rob the stockholders.

Chapter Twelve

RETURN TO THE BATTLEFIELD

Once back in San Francisco, he was greeted at the Bank of Italy's old headquarters on Clay and Montgomery by friends and associates in an office filled with flowers. They had not seen him for over a year and were shocked to find him looking so pale and exhausted. Both Belden and Bacigalupi hurried to meet him. They knew that Giannini intended to send a formal statement to the press and they tried to convince him to submit it to J.P. Morgan for possible censorship. They were doing everything possible to keep the true story from getting to the public. This finally confirmed in full his persistent suspicions that the House of Morgan was behind the lethal raids against his stock since June 1928.

He decided not to expose his intentions too clearly and issued a guarded statement to the journalists: "Those interested in Transamerica's affairs will receive no opposition from me in any plan or plans they may be considering as long as they are equitable and, in my opinion, in the interest of Transamerica stockholders."[136]

At the key meeting on September 22, 1931, Giannini briefly appeared in the boardroom, submitted his formal, long-delayed resignation from the corporation to Bacigalupi, and announced he would take the fight to the board if the interests of the stockholders were not properly respected. Facing a hostile board, he was consistently out-voted, and his resignation was unanimously accepted, if "with regret." Out of fear or convenience, Walker's draconian plans, which essentially asked for an unconditional surrender, were approved; full endorsement was also given to a complete reconstitution of the board of directors from which Giannini was excluded, eliminating his last chance to control Transamerica.

The stage was set for the radical transformation of Transamerica. All the eleven California members would be soon replaced, with the exception of Bacigalupi and Pedrini, by directors from outside the state, in order to strengthen the national aspect of the corporation. Moreover, a new working partnership with the prestigious old Boston house Lee, Higginson and Co. was announced with the declared intent of contributing to the growth and prosperity of Transamerica. The press, in particular the *Wall Street Journal*, welcomed the end of Giannini control of his former billion-dollar company as "the best thing that could have happened to Transamerica" and called Walker's new plan "history-making."[137] In reality, Lee, Higginson and Co. was also the American bank of Swedish entrepreneur and industrialist Ivar Kreuger and his 12 holdings and 140 operating companies, all in desperate financial need. This merger was therefore far from being beneficial to Transamerica and Giannini was right to be very suspicious.

That same day, Walker set in print his radical intensions to the stockholders to abandon the nationwide branch banking project, sell the majority of stock, all its banking, insurance, mortgage, and securities companies, domestic and foreign, in a manner which, according to the management, would be advantageous to the stockholders and the banks themselves. In time, the Bank of America NT&SA in California would also be sold. Meanwhile, the Transamerica stock in this period went down to $7 (and later plunged as low as $2), with the assurance that the intrinsic value was higher. The day the letter with the "changes in policy" was received, A.P. decided there was only one way to go: take the issue to the people who had trusted him and built the bank's reputation with him.

He was going to fight as a simple stockholder out in the open, and not behind the closed doors of power. At the same time he arranged a meeting with his old non-Italian friend from the business community, Charles W. Fay, a former director of the Bank of America NT&SA and postmaster of San Francisco, along with a few San Francisco stockholders who expressed their fear for Transamerica's future and the urgent need to devise a necessary counteroffensive.

On September 26, 1931, they founded the Associated Transamerica Stockholders (ATS) and elected Fay chairman of the organization. They all proposed, as the only man capable of an active opposition to Elisha Walker, A.P. Giannini, who immediately signaled his availability to assist with advice and accepted its leadership. The newly founded committee represented the holders of 2,000,000 of Transamerica's 24,800,000 outstanding shares and informed the press they were against the disposition of stocks and assets without "due notice and approval" of the Transamerica stockholders.[138] The Bank of America NT&SA now had a new chairman of the board, Lynn P. Talley, who had significantly been recommended by the Comptroller of the Currency and therefore was in line with the policy of liquidation at discount prices suggested by Wall Street.

On October 1, 1931, this disturbing program was more strongly reasserted by Transamerica with the announcement of the debatable merger of Bank of America (New York) with Charlie Mitchell's National City Bank, officially due to the great decrease in deposits of the Bank of America. This plan proved to be more beneficial to competitors than to the Giannini faction because the merger was in fact carried out at bargain rates. Giannini was sure it was the National City that was in financial difficulties rather than the Bank of America. This marked a turning point, the first major concrete step in the dismemberment of Transamerica. The Association became aware that they had to act quickly and start one of the most dramatic and bitter proxy battles in American financial history.

The fight cost money and A.P. Giannini had to borrow $50,000 on his life insurance policy to pick up steam. Lots of voluntary contributions started pouring into the temporary office in the Phelam Building, from a few pennies up, to finance and orchestrate a massive counter-campaign. Transamerica was very reluctant to give the Association the list of some two hundred thousand stockholders, as formally requested, and to get some results they had to have recourse to lawyers. Thanks to Bacigalupi's strategic delaying tactics, it took until November 7 before the first letter signed by Chairman Fay was sent to the entire mailing list. It denounced the policy to sell the corporation's assets and openly declared that stockholders did not favor the reelection of Elisha Walker as an executive and a director. It also enclosed a blank proxy form to be completed in favor of A.P. and Mario Giannini as well as Charles W. Fay for the annual meeting that was scheduled to take place on February 15, 1932. By endorsing the letter, A.P accepted the leadership of the movement in order to seize control of Transamerica and defeat Walker's irresponsible program of liquidation. They had only four months to count on.

Most likely nobody will ever know the true reason behind Walker's plan. Perhaps he simply yielded to fear when he had a chance to examine Transamerica's books and lost his head in the worsening Depression, believing that the only solution was to unload as fast as he could assets that he considered of doubtful worth. However, it is hard to believe that such an experienced, knowledgeable chairman of the board as Walker and a president like Bacigalupi, who had collaborated closely with A.P. for a quarter of a century, waited for Giannini to cross the Atlantic to conveniently discover "the fundamental weakness" of the bank's structure. Others, including A.P. *in primis*, maintained it was a deliberate plot of the East Coast banks to undo Giannini's empire because he had become too big and powerful on the financial scene.

At the beginning, Walker and Monnet recommended a low-key campaign, focusing on the minority of stockholders holding the largest block of shares, but then decided to become increasingly aggressive, once they discovered that Giannini's name was still magic and could draw large crowds of followers. A slander campaign started on the part of Walker and Bacigalupi and dirt flew in all directions.

A sequence of letters followed with all kinds of accusations, including that of dishonesty, denouncing Giannini's extraordinary compensations from 1927 to 1929. These malicious accusations were promptly contested by real facts and figures.

It was well known that A.P.'s salary had long been $1 a year, but he did have a large expense account. Back in 1927, to compensate its founder for his years of unpaid service since 1919, Bancitaly had unanimously voted to grant him 5% of the annual net profit. The first year A.P. refused the compensation, and asked to transfer the funds right away to the University of California–Berkeley, for a Chair in Agricultural and Resource Economics. In 1928 and 1929 a special fund was credited to him, the largest part of which was used to benefit the corporation.

The last year, before retiring, he waived the payment due to him amounting to $3,500,000 because he thought it was too much and he did not need it. While the New York management was accusing him of reaping large bonuses, Walker, Monnet, and Bacigalupi forgot to specify that besides their high salaries they would receive, as per written agreement, more than 7% of the Transamerica profits.

Among the reciprocal accusations the Association protested the high operational costs, which had jumped from about $300,000 a year, under Giannini's administration, to $3,000,000 under the new management. What hurt him most was that the New York Bank of America, which it had taken him ten years to make into a financial giant, had in two years, under Walker, almost ceased to exist.[139]

Walker's men for their part rejected the charges of stock manipulations, accusing Giannini of being the only cause of the debacle and guaranteed in writing to make "no move to dispose of any of its holdings except in the accordance of the stockholders."

The next annual meeting for this purpose was called for February 15, 1932, in Wilmington; this was also an important occasion for the reelection of the Transamerica Chairman of the board. All the unpleasant rumors and scheming, which would have crushed any other man, seemed to energize A.P. since he was fighting a just battle for "principle" to save the banks he founded against the Wall Street conspiracy.

This new challenge did wonders for his health, granting a much greater therapeutic effect than all the specialized treatments he had had in Europe. Jim Bacigalupi, in the meantime, had become Elisha Walker's right arm in California and both behaved as if they had already won. Giannini, however, was becoming physically and morally stronger in his intent to unseat Walker, followed by an army of stockholders who had openly declared a lack of trust in the present management. Many of the stockholders, along with 6,000 employees and 1,800 bank board members knew A.P. either personally or by reputation. He had a lifetime of impressive accomplishments, and in those hard times, he was the only person they wanted in charge.[140]

A.P., like in the old times, traveled to every single county in California, attracting large and cheering audiences, along with Fay and J.P. Scampini, a young San Francisco lawyer, who had been in the Bank's trust department and had delivered most of the campaign talks. In front of four thousand people in the Civic Auditorium of Stockton, "Scamp" charmed his listeners by stating: "Do these two or three Wall Street bankers imagine we are a bunch of fools—200,000 California investors who will sit still in the face of a financial cleanout carrying the economic and political control of California to two or three persons in New York? Do you think they can get away with Russian methods in giving orders to their employees that if they do not dissuade stockholders from joining our organization they will be fired?"

They decided to lodge a legal complaint against Walker's team misusing their positions and connections to remain in power, running up telephone bills at the stockholders' expense. Walker and his team were denounced above all for harshly threatening their employees with removal if they had become members of the Associated Transamerica Stockholders. When loyalty to the old boss and founder was forbidden by drastic written instructions, the staff knew that something was definitely wrong. Their hearts were with Giannini and by the end of November the Associated Stockholders had received, according to Fay, 150,000 white proxies, which represented more than half of the stockholders.[141]

The tour of the state, with its many spontaneous meetings along the way, proved to be more and more beneficial to A.P.'s health, in spite of doctors' strict recommendations. The direct contact with so many people who still believed in him cured his body and soul and energized him, increasing his moral conviction and physical stamina. Storming through Sacramento, Stockton, Napa, Calistoga, Sonoma, Santa Rosa, and the nearby towns, he was pleased to shake hands as in the old times, call everybody by name, visit branches, greet customers, and invite them to leave their savings in the institution that was still fundamentally "sound." He constantly reassured them that by banding together they could win this battle and better times would be ahead. Everywhere he went, he would collect more white proxies in his favor in a friendly and trusting atmosphere. Thanks to Attilio, in December 1931 and January 1932 all of his Hollywood clients were readily convinced to sign the white proxies rather than the blue ones sent out by "the duly constituted authority." Walker had deviously eased Doc out of his New York directorship to Los Angeles, thinking that Doc and A.P. had a troubled relationship. The proxy battle instead brought the two brothers closer together than ever before. From that moment on, they had a unique trusting fellowship until Doc died in 1944.

At the end of December, a letter was sent by Bacigalupi and Walker to all the stockholders encouraging them, if in doubt on which action to take, to consult any bank in the community.

They deliberately omitted to specify that a letter had previously been sent by them to all the rival banks slandering Giannini and asking to help get more blue proxies to keep themselves in office. Moreover, A.P. found out that the Walker administration, with the stockholders' money, had engaged over one thousand proxy solicitors, whose task was to perpetuate the old guard in office.

He felt he had the moral duty to restore the previous prestige and prosperity to Transamerica Corp. after he made the great mistake of placing the wrong person in a position of trust and power. Giannini, along with Scampini, rushed to complete his campaign from Sacramento to San Diego, from San Luis Obispo to Los Angeles where thousands of people were assembled. Scampini wisely informed the people that Giannini had dared to double-cross J.P. Morgan and this was the reason they were now relentlessly wrecking the institution. He had been told from the very beginning that to get along with Wall Street he had to take orders and obey, which he did not do. It was therefore obvious that the entrance of Walker into Transamerica was a well-thought-out plot to dismember Transamerica from within. During these fiery speeches, A.P, a white-haired veteran of the earthquake and a seasoned leader, listened and nodded while the speakers reminded the audience that when he was in charge the stockholders always made money. His presence everywhere managed to instill optimism and self-confidence. His celebrated statement during the campaign was: "Put your money in any bank in California. Dollars at work create credit and credit creates business and business creates jobs." He was offering faith in America's future by bringing prosperity back to California. A.P. Giannini proved that it is practically impossible to defeat a man whom people believe in. Before the decisive annual meeting, a last letter was sent in January by Walker and Bacigalupi reiterating all kinds of accusations against Giannini, making him responsible for stock manipulations and suspension of dividends, rejecting any responsibility in revoking branch banking, or intimidating employees and fiercely defending the sale of Bank of America in the interest of the stockholders. The letter was concluded by highly recommending that only the proxy bearing the latest date counted. Therefore enclosed was another blue proxy, inviting stockholders to sign in their favor and return.

When Giannini found out that an additional "pressure campaign" had been started, he asked to attend. After the official speeches, A.P had the opportunity to take the floor and be so inspiring and convincing that he left with quite a number of white proxies, signed in his favor. Half-a-dozen meetings had also been held in the East, in New York in particular, bringing in a significant number of white proxies to counterbalance the two executives hired at $700 a month by Transamerica (with the stockholders' money) to give precise instructions to fifty additional solicitors east and west of the Mississippi.

By the end of December, the Bank of America was on the edge of total collapse, with thousands of depositors requesting to withdraw their savings. The unprecedented loss of an average of $3 million a day in deposits alerted the San Francisco Federal Reserve Bank, which called the two opposing factions in the attempt to reach an impossible compromise. While Bacigalupi hired bodyguards to protect himself and his family, convinced that their lives were in danger, Giannini hired armed guards to escort the sealed proxies to the East Coast by private railway car.

The whole institution was paralyzed by fear, suspicion, and a great deal of paranoia. Employees were harassed and intimidated by arm-twisting treatment to the point that Giannini informed the press of "the shocking and reprehensible policies of control" as a means of determining the result of what was intended to be a free election.

Giannini devised a brilliant strategy to protect Bank of America's employees. Since only the proxy carrying the more recent of the two dates would be counted on the assembly day, employees were secretly instructed to sign the blue proxies in favor of Walker right away, to avoid any intimidation, and then, at a later date, they could sign a Giannini proxy as well and send it directly to the ATS headquarters in San Francisco. This way only on February 15, 1932, would the Transamerica executives find out who voted for them or for ATS. The last days were frantic and no members of the "Association of dissident stock-holders" could sleep anticipating the final victory. Giannini had hired Senator Hiram W. Johnson to represent the Association at the Annual Meeting at Wilmington, Delaware, with Elisha Walker, along with Judge Hugh Morris, an expert in Delaware corporation law.

In the end, an overwhelming majority of the stockholders confirmed their loyalty to and appreciation of Giannini and vot-ed according to the constructive policies, with the firm intent "to return the control of Transamerica to California, its birthplace and congenial home." That final annual meeting in Wilmington on February 15, 1932, marked one of the most monumental feats in the history of American finance.

A.P. Giannini had defeated Wall Street as Henry Ford had done before him, standing out as the only two resolute pow-ers who could neither be unseated nor discredited.[142] Associated Transamerica Stockholders received 15,371,578 proxies, com-pared to the 9.5 million for Walker. Giannini was back at the helm of Transamerica, ready to direct the same indomitable en-ergy he had dedicated to building the bank in earlier years into saving what was left of the Bank of America. He was elected Chairman of the Transamerica board, Chairman of the Bank of America NT&SA board as well as president of Bank of America, agreeing to serve without salary.

Attilio became the head of the bank's executive committee, operating from the Los Angeles headquarters, Mario became senior executive vice president of the bank, and many loyal Giannini men were brought into the executive committee. Jim Bacigalupi and Armando Pedrini and other senior officers resigned before Giannini reached San Francisco.

Shortly after midnight when it became obvious A.P. had won an overwhelming victory, Walker and the others left for New York, where they cleared their offices, frantically taking their papers with them, and burning most of their compromising documents so as not to leave any traces behind of their corruption and mismanagement.

A lot of work had to be done not only to restore the finances of Transamerica but also its heavily tarnished image. The following day, Giannini commented on this extraordinarily inspiring and instructive victory with these words: "It shows after all that right is might and that when stockholders have right they should not be too coward to fight."

When Giannini arrived in Los Angeles at Union Station he was welcomed as a hero. Reaching the Biltmore Hotel, he was cheered by a thousand employees and stockholders, eager to thank him and shower him with praise. His return home to San Mateo was compared by the *San Francisco Chronicle* to the equally victorious one of Julius Caesar returning to Rome.[143] Even the *New York Times* had to acknowledge his unprecedented victory: "At the age of sixty-one, Giannini returned from retirement to wrest control of the huge holding corporation which he originally created from the men to whom he relinquished the management two years ago."[144]

Chapter Thirteen

BACK TO THE GOOD TIMES

On February 23, 1932, at 8 a.m., A.P. was already at his old desk at One Powell Street in an open space without partitions. He had sent a telegram ahead to San Francisco and his other banks in California requesting the dividers installed by Walker's men to be ripped out of the bank headquarters for his arrival. He wanted to work out in the open and concluded the wire with an optimistic touch: "Let us join together in rebuilding a greater bank in a greater America." The first two big issues to solve were to re-establish a working harmony, according to his old fundamental principle that his bank was an extension of his beloved family, as well as face the extraordinary debt of $135 million that Walker had contracted, during his slightly more than one-year management, at 7% interest.

Giannini aimed at being surrounded by loyal collaborators, animated by the same ethical principles, and needed to purge some of the banks of his enemies, like the Bank of America's regional headquarters in Los Angeles, considered by Doc "a hotbed of intrigue." Some humiliated themselves and asked Giannini in writing for forgiveness. Others accepted a salary reduction to apologize for not being faithful during Walker's tenure. In order to overcome the gravest financial crisis of 1932, and cope with the loss of $138 million in deposits in the last six months of 1931, A.P had to cut expenses by readjusting and reducing the salaries of his employees, according to their level, and decided to work for no salary himself.

His gift for leadership paid off right away. In March, he sent a letter to all the branch managers launching a four-month campaign with the common goal of increasing Bank of America's deposits by $50 million, which they successfully accomplished. Giannini was truly convinced that "depressions are the product of fear" while "prosperity is born of confidence."

In this spirit, he soon after devised a creative and successful "Back to Good Times Campaign," urging people to be positive and leave fear behind. It was a psychologically innovative, privately sponsored, public relations endeavor, which set in motion a remarkable series of uplifting initiatives in order to instill new faith and hope in his collaborators and in the public at large. He decided to produce colorful cardboard posters to be placed along highways and on streetcars, and initiate a weekly series of "inspirational talks" of fifteen minutes each on a variety of civic, political, and cultural subjects by well-known guest speakers, within a confidence-building program (including fine music), broadcast every Wednesday evening that proved to be very useful and encouraging. Giannini spoke on the radio himself to two million listeners and went back to his old methods of investing in advertising and, above all, of being in direct contact with people in order to talk and listen to them and their aspirations, and explain once more what Transamerica could do for each of them. He was offering faith in America's future and bringing back prosperity to California.

The most significant "Back to Good Times" campaign was Giannini's endorsement of the construction of the Golden Gate Bridge, a unique opportunity to restore the public confidence in the new management of Transamerica after its image had been heavily tarnished, as well as bringing enormous economic benefits to northern California with thousands of new jobs. Experienced ironworkers were required along with electricians, carpenters, cable spinners, divers, and other tradesmen. Every job required a special level of skill, both for the sake of the task at hand and for personal survival, in particular the undersea site clearance and foundation preparation. It took ten years to get the necessary authorizations and overcome all the legal issues and indifference of the government's Reconstruction Finance Corporation that allotted all the federal funding exclusively to the San Francisco-Oakland Bay Bridge.

It was only thanks to Giannini's bold, far-sighted vision and generous acquisition of the first $6,000,000 in bonds, that this titanic project, requiring seventy-five thousand tons of fabricated steel, could start in 1933. Later on, he decided also to purchase the remaining $32 million to ensure the completion of this dangerous and unprecedented endeavor. It would be the longest steel suspension span in the world and the most exquisite Art Deco monument, a symbol of human resilience defying time, greatly dignified in its simplicity and grace.

As a result, when in 1936 Cardinal Eugenio Pacelli, soon to assume office as Pope Pius XII, blessed the bridge in front of the whole awe-struck city, including its large Catholic community, Giannini shared in the public acclaim of Strauss's civic dream, thanks to his having co-sponsored a world icon, a testimony to the creativity of mankind. Besides being a marvel of engineering, a vital connecting link in the U.S. Highway 101 stretching from

Mexico to Canada, it stood out as a model of joint private and public sponsorship, a healing therapy in the midst of the most pervasive economic depression.

Bank of America's road to recovery did not stop here. It included another three-month campaign to increase deposits with a well-publicized tour, which included over four hundred branches and twenty-six thousand miles. The results were astonishing: from less than a million to $22 million in three months, and $50 million at the end of the next month. The key to his unique success was again the fact that A.P. had kept his indomitable pioneer spirit of courage and cooperation along with his constant aspiration to banking innovation. His ability to inspire confidence among his customers was recognized not only by the local press but also by the prestigious *Wall Street Journal*.[145]

Chapter Fourteen

UNDER SIEGE AGAIN

In spite of his personal success, throughout the summer of 1932 Giannini felt under siege from government authorities. He strongly resented that most of his former senior Transamerica executives in California and New York, such as Arnold J. Mount and Howard Preston, had formed a network of enemies eager to make his life impossible. Their treachery had been deviously awarded. They had been skillfully relocated in the most important Washington policy-making institutions and given prominent jobs after losing the proxy battle. By covering the highest strategic positions in the regulatory bureaucracy, they were better placed than ever to mount a strong opposition against him. A lobby of influential people, such as John Calkins and Eugene Meyer, were responsible for recommending these prestigious high-powered appointments.

John Calkins, Governor of the Federal Reserve of San Francisco (FRB), showed on several occasions his prejudice against and his disdain for Italians and had become Giannini's personal enemy, whom he dismissively called a *dago*. Eugene Meyer, a shrewd Los Angeles tycoon who had become a prominent figure in the political and financial scene in Washington as well as a talented chairman of FRB, had worked for Herbert Fleishhacker's Anglo-California Bank before opening his own investment firm on Wall Street and had maintained strong personal ties with him. Calkins, Meyer, and Fleishhacker were bound together in yet another diabolical conspiracy, spreading unhealthy rumors that the "Bank of America was in the worst shape of all western banks."

A.P. became increasingly aware that the same "Wall Street gang" was bitter about his victory over Walker and was still at work trying to take his empire away from him. These same institutions had previously been passive; they never tried to prevent Walker from pursuing his destructive policies, but instead they were hounding Giannini with persistent requests for a strategic plan on how to solve the huge debt issue of Transamerica. Moreover, the Federal Reserve Bank was reluctant to recommend Transamerica, planting seeds of doubt in Washington vis-à-vis its soundness.

To make matters even more complicated, thanks to Meyer's personal influence, Mount, Preston, and Talley had joined, at the highest levels, the Reconstruction Finance Corporation (RFC), a newly established federal agency, meant to promote economic recovery during the Depression. It became obvious something was wrong because the San Francisco RFC included representatives from Crocker First National and Wells Fargo but not one single representative of the Bank of America, even though it was the state's largest bank.[146]

In November 1932, the American people elected Franklin D. Roosevelt with a large majority out of disappointment with the Hoover administration and in hopes of economic recovery. A.P. was in attendance, and listened to his famous speech at the Commonwealth Club in San Francisco and had no doubt he was his favorite candidate. He had a private meeting with Roosevelt the following morning in his suite at the Palace Hotel and promised his secret support to the Democratic Party. Roosevelt on his part confirmed he would consult A.P. on any matter relating to banking business in California and seriously consider Calkins' resignation as governor of the SFFRB, after being informed of his harassment of the Bank of America.

Interestingly enough, Herbert Hoover too had appealed at the last minute for Giannini's support for the Republican party, but A.P. was clear and brief, underlining that all the people he had expelled from his organization had been appointed to "some place of honor" and therefore he was not ready to collaborate.

In the four months between Roosevelt's election and his inauguration in March 1933, a wave of panic initiated a new cycle of an economic downturn and depression. Banks were in great difficulty and all of them needed cash, including some of his own branches in the state capital. A.P. proved once more to be an accomplished leader, able to solve problems promptly and dispel malicious rumors. Since all flights had been canceled because of the bad weather, a private pilot was hired and the largest shipment of cash ever sent by plane—$5 million—was delivered to Sacramento in mail sacks in less than forty minutes. The tension eased right away after A.P. reassured the customers that they could withdraw their money if they wanted to, and in a few hours there was no trace of a run on any bank in the city. However, it was a clear sign of how easily depositors could lose faith in banking institutions and go back to hiding their cash at home.

The governors of Michigan and Maryland were the first to declare an eight-day banking holiday, followed by almost twenty more state governors, who decided to take emergency measures by declaring a banking moratorium to cope with the downturn in the economy. President Roosevelt himself, the day after his inauguration in Washington, which Giannini had been personally invited to attend, declared a three-day suspension officially preventing banks from paying out or exporting gold.

Behind closed doors, Treasury lawyers and Federal Reserve officials were frantically at work to provide the nation with new banking regulations. The Emergency Banking Act, approved on March 9, 1933, gave the President of the United States and the Secretary of the Treasury for the first time in American history the power to close banks, and unlimited authority to regulate financial institutions at their discretion: a real turning point that marked the beginning of the most contradictory era in modern banking history.[147]

Thanks to Calkins and his destructive initiatives, the Bank of America was considered "hopelessly insolvent" and not allowed, unlike the other banks, to reopen after he malevolently enclosed an old examination report that did not reflect the latest, considerably improved state but the worst financial stage of the proxy battle.

The Federal Reserve officials in San Francisco decided to refuse to certify the Bank of America as solvent, a most flagrant case of unfair interference. Giannini, however, decided in desperation to turn as a last resort to William Randolph Hearst in San Simeon, which proved to be the best choice for the political handling of the issue. He was one of the Bank of America's most valuable corporate clients and had endorsed Roosevelt's election through his newspapers. He knew that the failure to reopen the Bank of America would have been a major disaster for California and the whole Pacific Coast; he also knew how unscrupulous the Wall Street gang was, and managed with a number of critical telephone calls to get the necessary authorization that Calkins had tried to withhold just because he was strongly prejudiced against Giannini.

Fortunately the Emergency Banking Act provided special advantages for the Bank of America, which justified Giannini's political support of the New Deal. First of all, it gave national banks the same rights as state banks to open branches anywhere the latter were allowed to. This enabled A.P. to merge his Bank of America of California with his national banks, mainly the Bank of America NT&SA. Within a year he was able to consolidate his 423 branches in 255 communities, leaving him only with one state-chartered bank with eight branches, with the option to switch back with great flexibility from a national to a state-chartered system when needed.[148] Moreover, the act allowed A.P. to open branches in states outside California, which he did in Oregon and Nevada. Giannini welcomed the federal supervision on bank holding companies like his own Transamerica Corporation because he thought it would provide greater stability and control over possible corruption.

Immediately after Roosevelt swept California by more than five hundred thousand votes, A.P. tried to recover some of the substantial sums Walker had lost by taking immediate action against him and three senior vice presidents on charges of fraud and embezzlement. He also filed criminal charges against Nolan, Bell, and Hellmans, owners and principal stockholders of Merchants National, responsible for the staggering $25 dollars the Bank of America had lost by buying the Los Angeles bank. This amount had become an exponentially growing debt, seriously threatening the very survival of Giannini's financial empire.

They had been involved for years in self-lending activities and had altered documents to conceal these illegal loan operations, but they had been so far spared from prosecution. In spite of the indisputable incriminating evidence, every action against them was constantly postponed during the Hoover administration. Giannini's hopes to get some justice and unmask Nolan, Bell, and Hellmans also went unfulfilled during Roosevelt's mandate, because in the meantime, further compromising charges surfaced. A criminal indictment would have generated political issues with serious consequences and a scandal of major proportions in the Democratic Party of Southern California.

Giannini believed he had a moral obligation towards his customers and stockholders, but nobody in power chose to pursue the matter any further. Giannini's letters of complaint to the Attorney General and to the White House led nowhere. Finally in December 1933 Giannini received a letter from the Justice Department stating that nothing more could be done; the case was closed.

After being defeated at the federal level, he was also thwarted at the state level vis-à-vis Nolan and Hellmans, because they protected themselves by declaring bankruptcy; he managed instead to get $460,000—an insignificant award, when compared to the $35 million in losses the Bank of America had sustained—from his civil suit against Bell, who in the end committed suicide. Giannini did not have an easy time trying to assert his rights in a politically corrupt environment that was full of intrigues and enemies. Since he now had irrefutable evidence that Meyer, Calkins, and Fleishhacker had chosen him as a target and were united in a common plan, the Bank of America had to adopt a survival strategy at all costs. And his "boys and girls" knew as much.

A.P. supported the President with public statements and visited him several times at the White House. He seized every opportunity to defend the New Deal's legislative program against its most severe critics who were openly accusing Roosevelt of "a socialized government control."[149] Also during the dinner party celebrating the bank's thirtieth anniversary he spoke from New York to more than two thousand invited guests and their families over a live telephone and radio link in very uplifting tones, expressing his admiration of the president's leadership. When William G. McAdoo was elected U.S. senator, and his protégé J.F.T. O'Connor was appointed as Comptroller of the Currency, they proved to be very sympathetic to Giannini and were influential supporters of branch banking in Washington.

A.P. was a genuine admirer of Roosevelt and fully embraced his reform of the banking system. Many major Wall Street bankers such as J.P. Morgan and James Warburg were opposed to the increasing powers of the Federal Reserve Board in Washington over the twelve regional Federal Reserve banks, as an instrument of despotic authority. Bankers who were not part of the Wall Street establishment, like A.P., were in favor of limiting the influence of the New York financiers.

During Roosevelt's first term in office, the Banking Act was approved on August 24, 1935, in spite of a formidable coalition of conservative senators who tried to stop the bill and reduce the president's power over the federal reserve system. This specific bill is considered the most significant banking legislation approved since the historical Federal Reserve Act of 1913. The main goal was to create business stability and encourage economic recovery by transferring power from district reserve banks to the Federal Reserve Board, which was supposed to develop a much more active role.

The Banking Act transformed the Federal Reserve into a politically appointed body selected by the President and run by the Secretary of the Treasury, who over the years acquired ever more power and authority. Giannini did more than anyone else to counter the claim that the bill was against the interests of the country.

A.P.'s outspoken defense of the administration's legislative program was genuine, as can be seen from one of his powerful statements:

"It is true that one of the purposes of the Banking Bill is to lessen the authority of bankers to determine the monetary policies of the country, but it should be emphasized that bankers at large have had very little voice in the determination of such policies in the past. The group that has exerted the predominant influence has been the New York bankers. Personally, I would rather that this power be exercised by a public body in the public interest than by the New York banking fraternity ... The bill is not a radical document sprung from the brains of theorists, but deep rooted in twenty years of practical experience with the Federal Reserve Act as tested by the worst depression in history."

The administration was so grateful for A.P.'s support that Roosevelt himself wrote a letter of appreciation and invited A.P. to the White House for dinner on more than one occasion.

A.P. at this time was maintaining that "our nation as a whole is much better off than it has been in recent years" and on his part he single-handedly succeeded in restoring his bank to health, without fulfilling his primary objective of extending his branch banking plans. Towards the end of 1936, A.P. had applied to open several new branch offices. In Washington, J.F.T. O'Connor, since taking office as Comptroller of the Currency, had often shown his good will but he became gradually more cautious because of pressure from many independent Southern California bankers wanting to block the Bank of America's further expansion.

A.P.'s hopes were short-lived. By 1937, William McAdoo proposed in the Senate a bill that would permit, within the boundaries of the reserve district, branch banking across state lines. The interstate banking bill was vigorously challenged by a group of conservative opponents under the leadership of Leo Crowley, chairman of the New Deal's newly created Federal Deposit Insurance Corporation, who saw in McAdoo's endeavor a further decrease of state banking autonomy and a dangerous consolidation of power in the hands of the few. McAdoo in the end was unable to overcome the opposition and withdrew the bill; Giannini felt betrayed because he thought he deserved better treatment from the White House after he had done so much for the Democratic Party and the new banking legislation.

A.P. had managed to overcome the tribulations of the Great Depression, achieve full recovery and some modest growth, exploring new spheres such as automobile sales, financing by installments, a housing program, agribusiness, and the growing movie industry. The New Deal opened up all kinds of opportunities. Giannini expanded loans to small homeowners and made more loans altogether than any other institution in the United States between 1934 and 1940. Short-term credit was in demand but it was usually handled by over seventeen thousand independent finance companies at interest rates varying from 10% to 30%.

In the 1930s, almost 60% of the population bought their cars through monthly payments and the Bank of America gradually conquered this market by charging far lower rates than its competitors. By 1935, the automobile became an important source of income, thanks also to a vast advertising campaign in newspapers and radio spots, a strategy specifically devised by Giannini, who managed to outrank the competition. Interestingly enough, the Bank of America was second only to General Motors in financing car purchases in California, which became more and more affordable, thanks to specific installment plans.

The Bank of America had been seen as an intruder by granting small loans from $100 to $1,000 dollars since 1929 when it introduced, just before the Wall Street crash, a personal loan department. Now it was helping all kinds of people again, from fishermen to grape growers. Newcomers were startled to discover that the Bank of America was ready to assist them even with their dental bills. After laborious negotiations, an innovative three-way agreement was reached between the Dental Association, the patient, and the bank. Giannini also promoted jewelry, furniture, lumber, and the manufacture of leisure and sports clothing without ever neglecting the world of California farming.

John Steinbeck's *The Grapes of Wrath* and Carey McWilliam's *Factories in the Field* unfortunately portrayed the Bank of America—directly or by innuendo—as a land-hungry institution, ready to take over the farmers' properties after forcing them out. As a matter of fact, Giannini was not at all responsible for their difficulties; on the contrary he was always eager to promote agriculture, honoring his own roots, and find a positive solution to every issue, but sometimes he was forced, just as other banks were, to proceed with foreclosure, a step he always took very reluctantly. Evidence of Giannini's constructive attitude is the increasing numbers of farmers who came to the various local branches of the Bank of America either to deposit or borrow money.

All these small, personal loans grew from $750,000 to $12 million and were almost all repaid with no loss to the bank.

With a view to favoring small businesses, A.P. had designed a program especially for those people who did not usually qualify for open lines of credit and had been denied by banks in the past. In tapping mass markets, the Bank of America was able to enter the lives of millions of Californians, allowing them to improve their standard of living at honest interest rates while also offering efficient service.

Giannini proved to have maintained, also during the Depression, a rare psychological insight as well as unique entrepreneurial abilities to adapt new business methods to the aspirations of the so-called little people, including the children of immigrants like himself. Perhaps they too could share the American dream as he and his family had done. He would even donate $5 to the parents of a newly born baby to start a savings account for the future depositor. The clever and wise idea of the bank as a department store was taking shape, allowing the bank to become a friendly helper towards leading a better life. He was a man always searching for the means of distributing services in the easiest and cheapest ways possible.[150]

A.P. reserved a special attention for the movie industry because it had suffered substantial losses during the Depression. Hollywood, from Metro-Goldyn-Mayer to Warner Brothers, was in desperate need of financing. In 1930, A.P. authorized a loan to form a new production company that two years later became 20th Century Fox, becoming ten years later one of Hollywood's biggest studios. Equally memorable was the loan to David Selznick, a producer who resigned from MGM to start his own production company. A.P. sanctioned a loan of $1.5 million, which led to the production of *Gone with the Wind* and other very successful films.

Another beneficiary of the Bank of America lending policy in the same years was Samuel Goldwyn who opened a $4 million line of credit to produce *Wuthering Heights*, a box-office sensation, among other Academy-Award winning films. Not to mention the magic name of Walt Disney who, as we have seen, had managed with a $1.7 million mortgage from A.P. to produce his first full-length animated film *Snow White,* which marked a turning point in his career.

A.P.'s intuition and risk-taking policy in underwriting the dreams of gifted people in whom he believed, like Disney or Strauss, was one of the most characteristic features of his personality. He was impulsive and calculating at the same time, a man who loved work and a good fight, as well as a builder with no limit to his own dreams.

Even in the deepest recession, he profoundly aspired to expand his operations into still-untouched farming communities. Towards the end of 1937, he filed a formal application to open half a dozen branches with the Comptroller of the Currency in Gonzales and Pinole, two farm towns in Northern California; unfortunately, O'Connor, who had decided to leave the administration to join the Democratic primary in California, left without taking final action. Henry Morgenthau Jr., who was then appointed by the President as Secretary of the Treasury had no sympathy for Giannini and his aspirations. For months, Giannini tried to inquire about the status of the necessary pending permits but officials in the Comptroller's office refused to talk about it.

Morgenthau was an old, close friend of Roosevelt and from a very wealthy New York family of German background. Still young, he had the financial means to buy a thousand acres near the Hudson River and start farming. After the First World War he expanded his activities into dairy farming and bought himself a large Victorian mansion after working in the Hoover Administration. He became a neighbor and close friend of the President, holding state jobs from the time Roosevelt was a governor. He took over the United States Treasury even though he hardly had the prerequisites for the job; his knowledge of economics, business, and banking matters was very limited. He had entered the administration in 1933, when the President had placed an embargo of indefinite duration on the export of gold and the dollar had depreciated, by presidential proclamation, in relation to the English pound. After being the head of Farm Credit Morgenthau was appointed Secretary of the Treasury. His intent and conviction from the very beginning was to privilege small independent banks over large financial institutions.

Transamerica's net profit had increased to $8 million after A.P.'s return, and in 1933 it expanded to almost $12 million, with the declared intention on his part to resume distributing dividends in 1934. *Forbes Magazine* published in the same year a very flattering article suggesting a list of American financial leaders the President should consult for advice. A.P.'s name was prominently mentioned alongside those of Henry Ford and Walter P. Chrysler as among the most experienced businessmen who should form an advisory cabinet for the President.

Even though A.P. had backed Roosevelt and his new policy of financial government control without any reservations, he soon realized how slow the new agencies were in granting loans and how applications were ignored for months and then often denied. When possible, he went on expanding, concentrating on bringing little Western banks into the fold of San Francisco's great Bank of America National Trust and Savings Association (with 447 California branches) and Portland National Bank (with its 28 Oregon branches). Transamerica had also absorbed Nevada's First National Bank and made it the center of a group of seven state branches.

However, Giannini's system confined its expansion to its own state, keeping in line with the 1935 Banking Act. Transamerica had no access to those Eastern states where statewide branch banking was forbidden. He remained confident, being an irrepressible optimist, that "under a unified banking system … it will be possible to have the equivalent of an up-to date-central clearing house for the nation." Branch banking had proved to be a success in England and Canada from the horse-and-buggy days, and Giannini thought it "was held back in America now by horse-and-buggy minds."

For A.P., 1935 and 1936 were years of stability and recovery. He was able to carve out some time for his family and enjoyed playing with Mario's two young daughters, Anne and Virginia, during weekends and at Christmas, as well as with his beloved dog. Mario Giannini had become President of the Bank of America, a position that was well deserved, and the proxy battle now seemed a distant memory.

A.P. still believed that sooner or later branch banking would be seen as a national necessity because it offered convenience to customers, diversity of risk, and shifting of reserves to meet demands.[151] He openly championed Roosevelt's re-election in 1936, this time through a thorough media campaign. The result was a great success for the President and signaled an excellent year for the Bank of America. Through home-modernization credit and automobile financing, he reaped a substantial profit, unlike the other banks, and managed to end 1936 with 491 branches in California.

The years that immediately followed, however, started a trying sequence marked by vicious fighting, conflict of personalities, misinterpretations, and vendettas, as well as tragic personal losses. His second son, Virgil, died at the age of thirty-eight of hemophilia only a few hours after a severe fall at home. Giannini was then sixty-eight, and with a broken heart, he tried to find solace by working and planning even harder for his beloved bank.

By the middle of 1938, the Bank of America was recognized as the largest savings bank in the United States, provoking envy and opposition from small independent bankers who saw in it the embodiment of a financial monopoly. During the same year, the President had approved a campaign to fight the general stagnation of business and had asked for a thorough Congressional scrutiny of the "concentration of economic power in American industry." Without their realizing it, banks were slowly becoming paralyzed by administrative and legislative handcuffs holding back normal business activity.

Morgenthau, a very suspicious, insecure, and self-righteous man, used Roosevelt's new dispositions as a pretext to exert his power by a more vigorous and direct supervision of Bank of America. He had decided to take strong action by making a number of rules. He insisted right away that Bank of America take immediate steps to improve its financial stability either by "increasing its capital or by cutting its dividends in half." By July 1938, he decided that Giannini was not allowed to use current earnings for the purpose of paying dividends.

The overall national scenario was slowly but surely becoming quite a different world, dominated by endless miles of red tape. Roosevelt's original intentions were sound and positive. His broad purpose was to keep the great system of national banks free from outside influences and allow them to continue as independent local institutions. However, the Comptroller of the Currency showed that with the excuse of exercising control in the name of efficiency, he could manage to make Giannini's life very difficult, if not impossible.

The office of the Comptroller slowly became a lobby of individuals exercising an ever-growing authority and glorying in the fact. Morgenthau decided to write a confidential report to William Douglas, the new Chairman of the Securities and Exchange Commission (SEC), which heavily criticized the Bank of America's financial condition and aggressive management. His attitude was highly contagious. Douglas also decided to focus his attention on Giannini's Transamerica Corporation on the basis of some presumed financial irregularities. They agreed together on a full-blown investigation of Transamerica and Bank of America; and to assist the SEC, Morgenthau gave Douglas confidential papers he had obtained and the full authority to make "relevant portions" of information public. At the Treasury it was immediately felt that Morgenthau's approach was far too aggressive. When Giannini obtained a copy of the report he had the dramatic evidence that he was again under severe attack.

The Treasury was after him. The charges were numerous and varied. According to them, Transamerica did not have enough reserve capital and dividends were paid when they should not have been. Figures had also been misrepresented. The most striking episode worth reporting regards Morgenthau's attempt to take over the Bank of America. He sent a telegram, bearing the signature of Acting Comptroller Marshall Digs (he consistently tried to target Giannini indirectly, through third parties) forbidding the Bank of America from distributing its dividends to the shareholders, in the hope that they would conform to the instructions. If this had happened, Morgenthau would have been authorized to take over the administration of the Bank of America to calm any disturbance among bank depositors.

This coup d'état would have allowed a merger of the Bank of America and Anglo-California under a conservator, to the great advantage of the failing bank. Mortimer and Herbert Fleishhacker, Morgenthau's friends and accomplices, were respectively the Chairman of the Board and President of Anglo-California, a San Francisco bank that had been charged with "unsafe and unsound practices" because of its unauthorized use of $13,683,920.22 of credits for private use and because for years its interests were supported with R.F.C. money. According to the local examiners' report they should have been removed from a position of trust and responsibility in the bank. Instead the file was ignored or rather, once forwarded to the Office of the Comptroller of the Currency, it was consigned to the wastebasket. In this atmosphere very questionable people were protected and honest bankers persecuted and even accused of fraud. If these machinations had succeeded, the Fleishhackers would have solved all their financial troubles and surreptitiously covered their misdeeds. Instead, Giannini disregarded the telegram and proceeded to the distribution of the dividends, sticking to his fundamental principles and saving his own bank, without being aware of the danger.

Other attacks came from SEC over Transamerica Stocks. Giannini was even accused of "unfair labor practices" and the Secretary of the Treasury dug up a spurious old income tax case against A.P. and his wife Clorinda because of a donation amounting to $1.5 million to the Giannini Foundation of Agricultural Economics. After vicious and gratuitous accusations, Mario was spending more and more time in Washington at conferences and hearings in protest of the government invading areas that were exclusively the bank's concern.

Morgenthau would regularly replace all the people who did not fully agree with him. Marshall Diggs was suddenly replaced by Cyril Bruce Upham, who was hoping to carve for himself a brilliant government career by taking over the case of Transamerica. The Bank of America was repeatedly examined for months at a time and castigated because of its financial success and innovative policies.

It was a fight for power among rival government agencies and a personal attack against A.P. Giannini. He was never ready for compromise and this gained him many enemies among political opportunists and Washington bureaucrats. Thanks to his persistence and courage, a temporary injunction in favor of the Bank of America was issued, forbidding the SEC from publicly investigating Bank of America's private dealings with customers. Giannini never stopped pugnaciously fighting for the interest and privacy of his depositors and stockholders. The final victory was reached much later when he decided boldly to counterattack in the same way, "from the shoulders," as he used to say. He had had enough of seeing the Bank of America position publicly distorted in a concerted smear campaign. Giannini was now prepared to surrender the national status of his banks so that they could again become state banks to counteract the Inquisition-like agenda set up by Morgenthau and his colleagues. Such a threat intimidated the Treasury officials who finally decided to adopt a more conciliatory attitude.

Mario informed the new comptroller Preston Delano of their irrevocable intentions by telegram, and in the early months of 1940 was able to reach an acceptable agreement in Washington. Charges against the corporation were, however, only dismissed in 1947, after nearly eight years and forty volumes of depositions and testimony in the most thorough investigation in the history of the SEC. Meanwhile, the outbreak of World War II worked in favor of the Gianninis because Roosevelt shifted his interests to the defense mobilization program.

For A.P., times were changing for the better, favoring the expansion of his institution and his nerve-wracking persecution by the government was finally coming to an end. Unlike the majority of American bankers who maintained a passive attitude, Giannini never gave up fighting what he saw as an injustice, even if he had to fight alone. He tried in his own way to make people aware that banks and bankers were now tied to rules and regulations written and enforced by federal officials. These were inevitably jeopardizing the relationship between the depositor and the banker.

A.P. was one of the very few to have the tenacity to fight back and denounce a growing abuse of power. Even though he and Mario were victims of a destructive bureaucracy, they constantly maintained a positive building attitude, establishing, for example, an endowment to aid young bankers to become better public speakers; by so doing, their expansion and earnings were enhanced.

Chapter Fifteen

THE NEW HEART OF THE BANK OF AMERICA

By 1941, the bank had outgrown its headquarters at One Powell Street. Giannini moved into a new multi-million dollar white granite building located in the very heart of San Francisco's financial district, on Montgomery, between Pine and California streets. Unlike the opening ceremony two decades earlier, the dedication of the 300 Montgomery Street building on December 9 was a subdued event overshadowed by the looming war. On December 7, the U.S. station at Pearl Harbor, Hawaii, was attacked by Japanese bombs. The next day President Roosevelt declared war on Japan.

A.P. was seventy-one and still looking to the future with great hope and confidence. The executive staff had a great reverence for A.P. and thought that it was only fitting for his role and age that he have a private office on one of the top floors. The twelve-story building was a five-minute walk from the site of the saloon where the first Bank of Italy had opened thirty-seven years earlier. Clarence Cuneo, Clorinda's brother, had supervised construction. He had been an important member of the family since actively helping Giannini to rescue the gold during the 1906 earthquake and fire.

A.P. reluctantly tried the new office but he felt isolated and complained that it was "a gilded cage" with "everything but a canary" and no contact with customers. He did not want to be relegated to a location from which he could not see the action; he loved to greet people and be of help to anyone who asked for his assistance.

The joyous challenge of the move was chilled by the advent of World War II. Also, on December 19, Clorinda Giannini died after having a heart attack while she was sitting at the piano in her daughter Claire's home in San Mateo. One of the great chapters of A.P.'s life had ended. The two had been together for half a century and the old fighter was heartbroken. He had been a faithful and devoted husband all his life and after forty-nine years of marriage he felt lost and depressed without her. She had given him happiness, companionship, and love. It was as if a part of him had ceased to exist. He was inclined to sell his family home to fight his fear of solitude and move to an apartment in San Francisco. Eventually Claire and her husband moved in with him, and gradually he managed to overcome his grief and deep sense of loss although he kept a picture of Clorinda on his desk for the rest of his life.

In spite of his great sadness, A.P. tried to rebound, because there was a lot to do and nothing was more healing than work. He invested all his energies in helping to win the war through his institution and reach a lasting peace, the prerequisite for new prosperity.

California had overnight become a military hub, the last stop for almost everyone sent to fight the war in the Pacific. Unlike World War I, during which his bank had played a minor role in providing funds for conversion to wartime production on the Pacific Coast, during World War II, A.P. saw major tasks ahead. He envisioned a determined home offensive, new services for the people, and an improved information relationship with the public in the hope that they would better understand banking and its potential. Between 1940 and 1945, although A.P. had somewhat withdrawn from day-to-day operations, his institution still emerged as a major force in facilitating the enormous expansion of the shipbuilding and aircraft industries. Much of the financing for the construction of new shipyards came from federal grants—more than $400 million on the Pacific Coast. Yet the subcontractors hired by the large yards still needed extensive loans. Thousands of small contractors were suddenly involved in making parts for prefabricated ships, manufacturing machines, masts, and boathouses. One major facility, the Mare Island Naval Shipyard in Vallejo, employed over 1,900 prime contractors and 300 subcontractors spread throughout California, Utah, Colorado, and Wyoming, involving more than 25,000 workers.[152]

A.P. had known Henry J. Kaiser, one of the west's leading shipbuilders, since the 1920s and they got on well with each other. They were both sons of immigrants who came from modest origins and had risen rapidly to success. They were both dreamers and always ready to welcome new challenges. Kaiser received from the Bank of America a loan of $7.5 million to finance part of the cost of his new Permanent Cement Company in California that later played a crucial role in rebuilding the damaged airfields at Pearl Harbor in 1942 and provided most of the cement used in the construction of naval and air bases on the Pacific Islands throughout the war. Even though Kaiser had never manufactured a vessel in his career, he accepted the challenge of fabricating twenty-four merchant ships and received a $40 million order from the U.S. Maritime Commission, his main financier, as well as a loan from the Bank of America, his largest private lender. He accepted because he firmly believed in the possibilities of pre-fabrication and assembly-line mass production.

A.P was also happy to support firms that he had followed for many years, particularly during the Depression. That was the case with Solar Aircraft Company in San Diego. During the 1930s, they had barely survived by selling frying pans, thanks mainly to Bank of America strategic loans, and by 1939 with A.P.'s help, they converted to defense production. In the next five years the company secured federal contracts for $90 million. The Bank of America continued to help with the expansion, and by 1944 they were successfully manufacturing stainless steel exhaust manifolds for B-29 bombers. This was a success story that Giannini loved to remember.

A.P. was entering his seventies and he had planned a slower pace for himself, often saying, "I want to withdraw a little further, and leave more of the active leadership in younger hands"; however, he continued to play a leading role, pursuing his major policies to the point that he could for the first time in his life rival the major Wall Street banks in financing the exceptional growth of industry in California. He still expected to be "the family watchdog ready to growl … and bark … if I find any turning away from the ideals on which the institution was built."

At that time thousands of troops would appear almost overnight near any small town that was not at all equipped to cope with so many newcomers, who needed, among other things, to take care of their finances. For A.P., the issue was easily solved by opening new branches but his requests were constantly refused by the Secretary of the Treasury Morgenthau and his officials. To ease A.P.'s disappointment, the Treasury Department awarded his bank a citation for distinguished service in view of his many contributions, including the sale of $2.7 billion of war bonds and other federal securities, more than any other private bank in the United States.[153] A.P. discovered, however, a hidden clause in the 1935 Banking Act, allowing banks to open seasonal agencies in order to handle a temporary and unforeseen influx of people. This exemption had been devised in view of the two World Fairs in San Diego and San Francisco, but was perfectly in line with the new needs. When A.P. first inquired, Deputy Comptroller C.B. Upham sent a blunt answer stating that he did not like to see "the Bank of America use the war as a means of expanding the number of its branches." Nonetheless, A.P. decided to go ahead and instructed his branch managers to proceed to open temporary "installations" whenever and wherever military commanders requested them, without applying for any specific permission. He was merely providing a service requested by the U.S. military during wartime, therefore if the Treasury officials were critical of this new initiative they would have to deal with the commander of the base.

A.P. had an independent personality and played by his own rules, believing that they were for the benefit of the community at large. Unsurprisingly, his unorthodox and often autocratic banking methods raised concerns within and outside financial circles. Throughout his career, he did not let anyone thwart him; he would find new loopholes by which he could elude federal and state regulations in order to promote the growth of his empire.

During a single month in 1942, A.P.'s installations provided $14 million in salaries and cashed 220,000 checks for military personnel and support staff. He was firmly convinced that in times of war this essential service had to be provided and the Bank of America could do it promptly and well. In 1943, the

Treasury Department, still under the direction of Secretary Morgenthau, ended up approving, albeit reluctantly, all of A.P.'s fifty new *de facto* temporary branches because soldiers had to be paid in addition to their living expenses. After the attack on Pearl Harbor, 110,000 U.S. citizens of Japanese descent were removed from their homes and relocated, for the whole duration of the war, to camps in remote parts of the western United States for fear that they might be in touch with the enemy.

The United States was also at war with Germany and Italy and consequently Americans of Italian descent were looked upon with suspicion too, including Angelo Rossi, the three-time mayor of San Francisco, a fierce anti-Communist who battled corruption in the Police Department and was mayor when the city's two most famous bridges opened in the 1930s. Nevertheless, in 1942, he was accused of being a sympathizer of Mussolini and of making fascist salutes during the San Francisco Columbus Day parade. His political career was ruined. Additionally, some 600,000 Italian-Americans, most of whom were elderly, were classified as "enemy aliens" and some of them were sent to internment camps.

However, A.P. was always treated with great respect and was specifically requested by the Federal Reserve Bank of San Francisco to provide banking services to the camps of Tule Lake and Manzanar. He promptly agreed to establish part-time installations in those two camps to meet the needs of interned Japanese people twice a week. These services were in line with the policy he adopted throughout his career: to help people who had been ignored or neglected.

The very rapid growth of business and industry offered him unique opportunities for imaginative innovations. He never neglected the financing of small businesses, even as he became more involved in financing large corporations. The Bank of America had its own research laboratories like a great manufacturing industry. Hundreds of banking brains contributed skill and expertise, not only to testing but also to perfecting new ideas to encourage enterprise and develop new resources. They created facilities to meet the expanding needs of an adequate war program, ranging from planes to ships and guns; from electric power and petroleum to lumber and cement, just to name a few. This laboratory kept working incessantly, shaping the war and the postwar years to create scientific miracles that helped to make civil life happier and more prosperous.

All the new inventions of wartime—electronics, television, light metals—would be the basis of a better and more diversified Californian economy. It was a very stimulating time, which saw agribusiness being joined by a wide range of new industries and services in an expansionist environment, all of which invited Bank of America to make the most of its opportunities. The war had transformed California from a largely agricultural state into a rapidly growing industrial power.

When interviewed, A.P. would say: "Lots of new businesses will be opened ... Folks over the country want to settle in California. Jobs, I can't see any lack of them. We'll get bigger."[154] Moreover major social changes within the bank brought about some radical innovations. Since over 3,500 employees—out of about 9,800—had to join the army during World War II and at the same time the demand for services had dramatically increased, Giannini hired over 11,700 women to replace the men at war, successfully meeting a unique challenge and drastically increasing the nation's female workforce. He had a deep respect for women. He considered them life-givers but also valuable, loyal workers and intelligent collaborators.

Along with California's governor Earl Warren and other bullish major industrialists such as Henry J. Kaiser, A.P. in 1945 truly believed that California was "the heart of a great new empire and an area of unbounded possibilities."

Among the new opportunities was subcontracting: a practice that stimulated manufacturing on the Pacific Coast through the assembly of pre-fabricated parts for ships and aircraft. Thousands of small business enterprises delivered their parts to large assembly centers. In this way they were performing a very meaningful patriotic task by converting their plants to national defense while ensuring the vital functioning of local decentralized industry. However, as these small businesses converted to war production and secured government contracts, they needed local loans. To facilitate more war contracts for small businesses, in 1941 A.P. established a Bank of America Defense Information Office in Washington, D.C., inside the Mayflower Hotel. Its staff regularly solicited work for California's subcontractors and in particular for clients of the Bank of America. During the first six months of operation, the office received about two thousand such contracts, totaling $42 million. This experience convinced A.P. that a permanent government office to perform such functions would be very useful. By 1942, the War Production Board established a division to direct federal contracts to small businesses, which proved to play a positive role.

A.P. never gave up the impulse to educate his customers by making them aware of these new options. In the same year, he convinced the Governor of California, Culbert Olson, to hold a conference in Sacramento in order to promote local subcontracting and at the same time was actively engaged in a local campaign, through its branches, to promote adoption of these ideas, organizing small pools of manufacturers who would qualify for federally guaranteed loans.

The war brought in thousands of new residents and profoundly altered the state's economy. Before 1940, agriculture had attracted people to the state. After Pearl Harbor, people arrived looking for jobs in war-related industries.

The development of new wartime manufacturing thus caused another major population boom in the West. By the end of 1941, California's population had increased by more than 400,000 and the number would drastically increase each year of the war. Cities like San Diego doubled their population and Los Angeles grew by 800,000 newcomers from other parts of the country because of the aircraft plants' need for skilled labor. A survey of Los Angeles at the end of 1943 revealed that one out every four people had arrived in the city in the two years following the nation's entry into the war because Los Angeles had become the major arsenal, incessantly turning out planes from aircraft companies such as Consolidated, Douglas, Lockheed, and North American. The San Francisco Bay Area became a conglomeration of boomtowns because of shipbuilding. Richmond in particular expanded from 20,000 in 1940 to 160,000 in 1943.

This extraordinary influx of people from all over the United States created a housing shortage never before seen. People were sleeping in campers, trailers, and even in the open. In spite of the fact that 100,000 new housing units were granted, many more people needed homes, giving the Bank of America additional opportunities to expand its operations. Since between 1940 and 1945 the demand for new home construction was soaring as a reaction to the continuing movement of people into the state, the bank granted almost one million loans guaranteed by the

Federal Housing Administration Act, and therefore with almost no risk to the bank. Most of these credits were to provide housing for war workers. All this created a major boom in the economy, placing a terrific pressure on banking services.

Bank of America branches operating in small towns on an average of $15,000 cash availability were all of a sudden handling deposits and loans in the hundreds of thousands, and sometimes even in the millions of dollars.

Giannini decided, in the spring of 1942, to purchase a score of national banks, which he would then convert to state-chartered banks, freeing himself from the direct supervision of the Treasury Department, which of course infuriated its officials. In particular, he bought the Citizens National Trust and Savings of Los Angeles with the permission of the Federal Reserve Board, without them realizing it already had thirty branches of its own.

The supervising federal institutions were opposed to Transamerica's further expansion either directly or indirectly. Marriner Eccles, the feisty Utah-born chairman of FRB who had been very appreciative of Giannini's contribution toward the administration's victory during the Roosevelt administration, had now turned very rigid and critical, and managed to convince the three regulatory agencies to take a uniform policy that would restrain Transamerica's further expansion and impose disciplinary action, if necessary.

Giannini was convinced that he had been persecuted and discriminated against in his attempt to extend his services where they were needed. He thought that in the current American system of free enterprise these methods of dictatorship were misguided. The federal authorities kept praising him for his abilities as a branch bank operator but condemned his methods of expansion. An informal agreement was reached between Giannini and Eccles in Washington on the condition that all the other banks or holding companies were also prevented from expanding, but the truce did not last long. When Giannini found out that the freezing measures were being applied only to his institution he no longer felt bound to adhere to the terms of the "stand still" agreement. The reality was that Chairman Eccles had singled out Transamerica and Bank of America for criticism and remained firm in denying Giannini additional branch permits. A.P. decided, once again, to defy these intrusions, which he thought to be highly detrimental to the very life of his institution. In 1945, when Japan surrendered, Bank of America had 492 branches, three less than when the war started. So he had to invest $8 million to enlarge the existing branches, located in the most populous communities, trying in this way to cope with the long lines of customers from neighboring communities in which permission to open branches had been denied.

On May 6, 1945, which marked his seventy-fifth birthday, Giannini made another of his grand gestures. By announcing his resignation from the Bank of America he handed over the chairmanship of the board and accepted the honorary title of Founder-Chairman.

The same year, the Bank of America had become the largest privately owned bank in the world, surpassing Chase National by $72 million, with assets of over $5 billion. Even the Wall Street bankers who had scorned and attacked him in the past had to recognize that immigrants, farmers, tradesmen and women, as well as soldiers, could be valuable customers and that small deposits could generate big profits. A.P. had proven to be a master in creating a broad base of four million customers from all walks of life.

In the same year, Roosevelt died and Morgenthau resigned as Secretary of the Treasury. Giannini took the occasion to apply to the Comptroller of the Currency Delano for permission to open thirty-five new branches but only two of the applications were approved after more than six years of waiting.

Delano was inclined to be generous but Eccles was strictly holding to the terms of the so-called freeze agreement. As soon as World War II ended, Giannini was eager not only to increase the economic prosperity of California that had rapidly turned from an agricultural state into a growing industrial power, but also to rebuild Italy's devastated economy.

He always felt close to the country of his ancestors and therefore flew to Italy to inspect the *Banca d'America e d'Italia*. With its thirty-one branches and assets of $30 million, the Italian branch had survived very well under the Fascist regime and was in a position to become the leading lender for the reconstruction and quick recovery of Italy's economy. A.P. also made sure his bank participated in the Marshall Plan, which provided loans to the Western European countries devastated by the war.

Some people thought the end of the war would mark a return to hard times and economic depression. Giannini instead had a great hope in the future and would optimistically state: "The West Coast hasn't even started yet." He believed that all the inventive products manufactured during the war would now be produced for peaceful purposes and become more affordable and functional.

Giannini at that point was also ready to expand globally. The most natural start was to expand into the Pacific area and the Far East. Stephen Bechtel, a top California industrialist, had urged Giannini to open a branch in the Philippines, and try to bring order and prosperity to the economic chaos of postwar

Manila. The branch was very successful and in three years it became the fourth-largest bank in the country. A new branch was then opened in Bangkok and later on in Shanghai. Even though Japan had been a fierce enemy during the war, the United States helped the country to recover and Bank of America opened branches in Tokyo, Kobe, Osaka, and Yokohama.

The immediate postwar years were marked by a pronounced dichotomy between the economic triumph of the Bank of America, recognized and praised by the press and the public at large on one side, and on the other the worsening hostility of the FRB because of Eccles, who reached the point of officially bringing antitrust charges against Transamerica Corporation. He was so intolerant that he even dreamed up what everybody recognized as an "anti-Giannini bill,"[155] proposing to place all bank holding companies under the direct control and supervision of the FRB. Giannini was not opposed to restricting legislation in principle, provided it was applied with no discrimination.

A.P. continued to buy banks through Transamerica. After Morgenthau resigned, Fredrick Vinson was appointed Secretary of the Treasury and after him John Snyder, a close friend of Truman and a very accomplished civil servant. Eccles was exasperated for more than one reason. Giannini had received the good news that the Transamerica hearings had finally come to an end after eight years and his application for over 15 new branches in California had been approved. Moreover, as of 1947, Transamerica Corporation controlled some 41 banks with 562 branches in California, Washington, Oregon, Arizona, and Nevada.

Bank of America's network of offices in California alone accounted for 500 branches. The corporation's total assets exceeded $7 billion.[156] Eccles was disappointed not to be reappointed by Truman as head of the board but was offered instead the position of vice chairman. Everybody was surprised that he accepted the demotion. The relationship between Truman and Eccles became increasingly strained and in the end Eccles was transferred back to Salt Lake City. In spite of, or maybe because of this, he relentlessly continued to pursue Transamerica and the Bank of America. In 1948, after years of charges and countercharges he managed to put Transamerica on trial, charging the corporation with monopolization and antitrust violations under Section 7 of the Clayton Act. This discriminatory harassment only made A.P. fight harder, think faster, and battle longer. As he himself stated: "If my opponents had not forced me … unless they pushed me from behind, I would have never pushed ahead."

A.P. never saw the happy ending of this unfortunate prolonged attack. In fact, it was only in 1952 that the U.S. Court of Appeal finally rejected the board's antitrust verdict against the corporation. Not even Mario came to know the final outcome, as he died that year, before the verdict was in, at the age of 57. Claire Giannini Hoffman, who took A.P.'s seat on the bank's board of directors, was the only member of the family who could rejoice in this victory, which turned out to be less than complete. On the one hand, the board of the FRB was once and for all defeated and humiliated because it did not succeed in proving its charges of monopolization. On the other, Congress passed a bill stating that a holding company could not own more than one bank. As a result Transamerica had to divest itself of all banks except the Citizens National of Los Angeles and gradually dissolved because of internal issues, which would never have occurred during Giannini's lifetime.

The Bank of America remained intact, while other units were severed and finally even the Citizens National of Los Angeles merged with the Crocker National Bank of San Francisco. All the same, Giannini's legacy remains vibrant and meaningful. It came from the heart of an enlightened man who was far ahead of his time. He was identified with the legendary figure of Aladdin and his magic lamp could fulfill every true wish. His vision was larger than life because he had innovative ideas and the courage to try them out. His desire to expand was due mainly to his aspiration to bring services to the people, wherever they was needed.

During the early spring of 1949, despite his declining health, Giannini spent much of his time with Transamerica lawyers getting ready for the public hearings initiated by FRB against his corporation. According to his old strategy, he intended to go directly to the people and bring in over 1,600 witnesses, testifying that the Bank of America was conceived as serving people in a way that no other American bank had done before.

Giannini had become the founder of the world's largest private bank and therefore one of the most powerful people in the world, but he remained a modest individual who did not want to run the risk of joining the millionaire class. He was reported to have said on many occasions: "No man actually owns a fortune; it owns him." To prevent this danger, in October 1945, at the very end of the war, he decided to allocate half of his assets, in the amount of $509,235, to the newly founded Bank of America Giannini Foundation, a nonprofit corporation providing educational scholarships for his "boys and girls"—Bank of America employees—and to promote scientific research in the field of medicine. He considered the Bank as an extended family with himself as a benevolent leader. He left precise instructions to his son Mario, who was the executor of his will: "… Administer this Trust generously and nobly, remembering always human suffering … Like St. Francis of Assisi, do good—do not merely theorize about goodness. This is my wish and I confidently commit this Trust to your hands for fulfillment."

Even after donating half of his fortune to the trust fund, he was always ready to share because he believed in collective wealth. Despite having no formal education, unlike his brother who was a graduate from Berkeley, he nurtured a deep respect for learning and self-improvement. On the other hand, he believed that "a lot of people working together can create a lot of wealth for a lot of people. But one man who works selfishly for his own wealth at the expense of others creates nothing worth having. He generates poverty. There's poverty in his mind, in his heart, and in time it will show up in his pocket."

His personal vision of capitalism was very positive and basic. It was based on the simple concept that business needs capital and that whoever saves something and puts it to work is a proto-capitalist. In this perspective, capitalism becomes democracy at work, worth pursuing collectively. His vision was intergenerational and centered on sharing; his social revolution sprang directly from the heart, from a love for the unprivileged, the poor who had left their native countries in the hope of building a better life for themselves and their families. This was the main reason he managed to change the lives of so many people with lasting results. He firmly believed in making capital of young Americans because he thought it was "the only good crop where the land has never failed us, year after year."

In the San Francisco earthquake and in the two World Wars the Bank of America was seen at its best, demonstrating a rare ability to grow through its willingness to explore every possible way to help other people. The state and the bank prospered together, and together came of age. In the process, the Bank of America played a huge part in the maturing of the California economy, more than any other institution except perhaps the United States government.

Chapter Sixteen

GIANNINI'S LEGACY

On May 6, 1949, A.P. celebrated his 79th birthday at home in San Mateo with his son Mario, his daughter Claire, and a few close friends. It was the first time he had not marked the day at the office with flowers and cake. He let his employees know that on this occasion he wanted to spend a quiet day with his immediate family.

His life had been rich in accomplishments but also a demanding and draining one. He had lately become more conciliatory towards everybody and in recent months went into work less often because of heart trouble and chronic bronchitis. He knew the bank was safe in Mario's experienced and wise hands, but his compassionate personality and booming voice were missed at 300 Montgomery Street.

Less than a month later, suffering from a bad cold, he was taken first to St. Luke's Hospital and then, when his condition worsened, to Mills General Hospital. By May 28, he was feeling better and was released by his doctors. He was happy to be back home in the more familiar surroundings of San Mateo, and hoped to return to the bank within a week. In the unpretentious house at Seven Oaks that had been his haven for many years,

A.P. died in his sleep of heart failure on Friday morning June 3, 1949. With him were his doctor, a nurse, Claire, and Mario.[157]

At Giannini's death, the Bank of America was globally recognized as the largest private bank in the world. He left behind 517 branches and more than $6 billion in assets. His personal estate, however, was valued at only $489,278, of which he left $50,000 to assorted charities. He never collected any valuable art or antiques but lived humbly in the same suburban enclave, intentionally avoiding the glamour of San Francisco society. When his will was filed on June 14th, everybody was surprised to learn that a man of his eminence could leave such modest personal assets. In real terms, he was worth less when he died than before he founded his bank. He left the balance to the Foundation, which he never considered a cold corporate entity but rather as *la famiglia*, eschewing formality and embracing loyal colleagues, who had worked alongside him, sharing his ideals for the last forty years, as his extended family. This is entirely consistent with a revealing answer he gave to a reporter who asked him what in a nutshell was his philosophy about money. His simple answer was: "I believe in a more general distribution of wealth and happiness." He was a doer and a builder, not for himself but for a global community.

He knew that the bank had to make money to justify its existence. However, only by remembering that money represents the dreams and aspirations of human beings was A.P. able to build what he did. He fought to construct his empire not out of the desire to become rich and powerful or to acquire personal glory, but because he was convinced that branch banking, his lifelong goal, was an enduring and efficient way to provide people with a convenient service. In his retirement years he often repeated: "If

I ever hear that any of you are trying to play the big man's game and forgetting the small man, I'll be back in here fighting."

At his death, tributes poured in: The *New York Times* stated outright that "no one has had a greater influence in the history of California"[158] while the *Los Angeles Times* recognized that "his unorthodox methods have been much criticized, but also much copied. That he changed banking in his state—if not in the nation—can never be denied."[159]

He was as important as Morgan, Vanderbilt, and Rockefeller but he was unique in his profound interest in the average American. If J.P. Morgan personified banking for the wealthy classes, A.P. symbolized banking for the masses. A.P. related to the underdogs of the world. In spite of the power and importance he attained later in life, he always perceived himself as one of the little people. To him, banking was a noble job that allowed him to help common people reach their dreams, step by step, and in so doing, he achieved his own.

Giannini's funeral took place on June 6, 1949, at St. Mary's Cathedral in San Francisco. A.P. had been a life-long Roman Catholic and Archbishop John J. Mitty conducted a requiem mass attended by an exceptionally large crowd. More than 2,500 people filled the cathedral. Thousands more lined the streets outside to witness the funeral procession. He was buried in a private burial service not far from his home, at the Holy Cross Cemetery in Colma, next to Clorinda, the love of his life. In keeping with A.P.'s wishes, all Bank of America branches around the world remained open all day, serving people.

Epilogue

My aim has been to sketch the portrait of one of the greatest men of his time, the father of modern banking, and the catalyst of a peaceful social revolution.

He will be remembered not only because he was the founder of the Bank of Italy (1904)—later renamed the Bank of America (1930)—but because he was a man of vision, ahead of his time and unique in his evangelical generosity. He was a warm, compassionate, self-made man, a dreamer and a doer at the same time. A.P. was part of an immigrant community based in the far West, initially distrusted and neglected by society and the existing financial establishment. From his adolescence he was outspoken and gifted with a strong business instinct, an indomitable will, and a fighting spirit. Being of humble origins and with little formal education, he wanted constantly to prove himself by excelling, by being the best, and he inevitably became a point of reference for everybody who was interested in self-improvement. He believed in the American Dream but did not want to selfishly realize it only for himself. He was willing and eager to share it, along with his rare entrepreneurial talents.

At the age of thirty-four, Giannini, already a successful merchant on the waterfront of San Francisco, turned into a banker by accident rather than by design. With the original approach of an outsider, he devoted his life to making a bank which, without excluding the rich and powerful, would privilege ordinary folk, especially the Italian immigrants who were arriving in San Francisco and settling in North Beach penniless, unemployed, and ignored by other banks. His unique "people's bank" was his brainchild and a part of his soul.

A.P. discovered he had a vocation to fulfill; he followed his inner voice in helping not only people of Italian extraction but also of other backgrounds to settle in California, because he was convinced that their presence and work, once they had mastered the English language, would ultimately enrich his native state, which in the first half of the twentieth century became one of the fastest-growing regions in the nation.

Was this some kind of utopian dream? William Butler Yeats maintained that "it is in our dreams that our responsibilities begin." Giannini was not the first believer in realizable utopias. Utopian thinkers have existed throughout history from Plato in ancient Greece to Thomas More in Renaissance England. Utopias are usually generated by dissatisfaction and the need for change.[160] Giannini was deeply concerned by the way banks were run in the first decade of the twentieth century. His discontent led to a revolutionary change of approach promoted by himself and a small group of enlightened people, including his stepfather, who shared the same vision and values. Giannini's missionary energy carried him beyond wishful thinking the moment he was able to take action and make the irrevocable decision to open his own bank. He did not limit himself to imagining the future: he helped to create it.

Giannini's first utopian act was to try to change the mental attitude and behavior of the directors of the Columbus Savings and Loan, who were used to serving almost exclusively themselves and their wealthy and powerful customers, but after trying persistently at various levels, he realized it was an impossible task.

Unlike his competitors, he wanted above all to improve the living conditions of the hard-working immigrants who had recently landed in the Bay Area. However, far from withdrawing in passive resignation, he bravely and strategically intervened to persuade a select group of people to pursue the radical social change he wanted to achieve. From that moment, his considerable power of persuasion and exceptional ability to motivate his collaborators made his utopia achievable. He received the unconditional consensus of his newly established board. His bank became a unique institution (he used to call it affectionately "my model child"), which was so vigorous and progressive that it soon left its competitors behind. He taught children the virtue of saving; he increased the number of women customers, and—more radically—of women employees, giving them the same dignity and the same salary as their male colleagues.

His bank kept its doors open in the evening and on weekends to accommodate his new customers. A.P. and his staff spoke their language, remembered their faces and names; they taught them patiently how to fill out forms, accepted small deposits, and offered loans at the lowest-possible rates because his purpose was not to become rich but chiefly to provide a service to a growing community and help it become prosperous and integrated into the American way of life.

He was on the same wavelength as Father Raphael Piperni, his far-sighted friend and spiritual mentor at St. Peter and Paul's, the Italian Catholic cathedral *par excellence* of San Francisco and the West, a reassuring haven for the Italian community that retained much of their home culture while promoting a real dialogue with the host country. This church performed a key social role; in fact, the very first Americanization School in California was founded there, which was immediately in great demand and for years enjoyed a remarkable success.

As in Giannini's vision, Italian immigrants would no longer be considered second-class citizens in their adopted city but full Americans who continued to treasure their remarkable heritage, including their culinary traditions. When A.P. opened the Bank of Italy in the center of the Italian community of North Beach, at lunchtime he would not go home to San Mateo or to a fancy restaurant. He would stay in the area and go to "Da Maria" on Columbus Avenue, an informal family-style hangout in the unpretentious apartment of a talented Italian woman who made a living by cooking traditional Italian food. In the living room, one long table would accommodate about twenty people, on a first-come-first-serve basis. Giannini was a regular customer and would unassumingly sit next to a carpenter or even another banker. Everybody wanted to be there because of the authentic Italian food. He also had Emilia at home in San Mateo who would maintain Italian traditions in the kitchen while helping out Clorinda and their eight children.

Giannini, like Father Piperni, wanted to build the best society for the most people, socially integrated yet proud of their heritage. He was able to think outside the box and lived free of any illusions of self-regard.

He tried to retire at least three times but was compelled to come back to rescue the bank from deliberate mismanagement. He was always ready to make room for younger people by encouraging generational turnover but his generous nature made him too trusting on occasions and in his professional life he came to experience the bitterness of disloyalty.

The only love affair he had, besides with his wife, was with his dreams and the dreams of other people. He truly believed that America, especially California, was a land of unmatched resources and opportunities, as well as a social and economic powerhouse of enterprising people from all walks of life.

He loved nature and chose to live in the countryside, among oak trees and flowers. Every morning before going to work he dressed elegantly as befitting a leader, giving due dignity and respect to his work, picking a carnation from the garden and putting it in his lapel. He loved his white Sealyham terrier because the dog brought some carefree joy into his demanding everyday schedule.

He had eight children and lost six of them during his lifetime; only Mario and Claire outlived him. Some passed away in their infancy, some in their adolescence like Lloyd Thomas, who died at 14, and Virgil, who died at 38. They all died of hemophilia, a hereditary blood disorder, which was a constant lethal threat hanging over his head and those of his children, like the sword of Damocles.

Throughout his life, death would relentlessly knock at his door, becoming a sort of metronome stressing the fleetingness of human existence. After Virgil suddenly passed away in 1938, A.P. was devastated by the loss of his child and found some consolation in long conversations with Father Piperni, his kindred spirit at St. Peter and Paul's. Despite so many trials, A.P. became spiritually stronger.

He had a remarkable ability to overcome challenges and difficulties with endurance and faith. He never forgot, in spite of his losses, to be humbly thankful for what he had received and never gave up dreaming and helping other people get a step closer to realizing their dreams. He wanted to be near people and to serve them, especially the ones most in need. After the 1906 earthquake, anyone who wanted to rebuild San Francisco would line up and get from his improvised bank on the wharf the cash they needed and would leave with renewed hope. Later on, during the Depression, he was a positive and encouraging leader, insisting that California, the United States, and the Bank of America were headed toward a better and greater future. He transformed every calamity into an opportunity. Being a keen listener and observer he was interested in finding out what his customers' aspirations were and helping to achieve them whether they wanted to open a farm, buy a car, build a bridge or make a film.

A.P.'s granddaughters Anne and Virginia, his son Mario's children, are the only surviving members of the family to have known A.P.'s greatness firsthand. I had the privilege of meeting them in Anne's beautiful apartment in San Francisco in January 2017, and they were both able to provide a wealth of information, especially about their grandfather's private life and habits. Anne, the elder of the two, had vivid memories of A.P., in particular of a major trip they took together to Argentina across the Andes and the Pampas in July 1947. During that journey to South America two years before he died, he wanted to get closer to his young granddaughters. He would challenge and engage them by getting them to translate the local newspapers from Spanish into English for him. He believed in handing down ideals of motivation, discipline, and self-improvement, and he tried to communicate these values and goals to younger people, starting with his immediate family.

Giannini was American-born but never forgot where he came from. He never turned his back on who he was. He was proud of his Italian heritage and had a great respect for Italy's past in the arts. His close ties to Italian immigrants, through his parents, his stepfather, and his father-in-law played a prominent role in A.P.'s view of the world.

He had a real feeling for the people from Italy who worked hard in the vineyards, in fishing, and many other sectors. He never tried to hide his background but would rather highlight it. He brought in a seed of "Italian spirit and creativity" at every level and believed in interaction and understanding.

Giannini's primary concern was always his own America, his own people, his native California. He was sincerely ecumenical and for this reason he also financed the Episcopal Grace Cathedral on Nob Hill because of its special role as a community church beyond denominational distinctions. His contributions, often anonymous, were very generous to every creed. He was a convinced member of the Catholic community, yet open and respectful of all other faiths. A.P. had the occasion to meet the highest representatives of the Catholic Church, such as Cardinal Pacelli, future Pope Pius XII, and was given the most prestigious recognition from the Vatican.

He was aware throughout his life he was a member of a minority, in the midst of a WASP establishment, but this became more a source of strength than a liability. He knew he was different and was proud of it. Towards the end of his life he used to say: "I give the bulk of credit to my enemies. They stimulated me. They kept me going. I am thankful to them."

There is still magic in Giannini's name because he was unique in his endeavor to build a social utopia, and he managed to improve California, if not the United States as a whole. Virtually every Californian to this day has benefitted from Giannini's concern for the state and its people.

His innovative and all-encompassing approach to banking and his constant introduction of new practices and services allowed him to rise to the very top and become an outstanding example of the American success story. His bank revolutionized modern banking by introducing installment payments and later the credit card (called BankAmericard in 1959 and Visa in 1975), thus creating an increasingly wide market in consumer goods for borrowers who had no other source of credit. Today, the Bank of America has more branches and ATMs than any other bank in the world, true to Giannini's lifelong mission.

A.P. believed that a private enterprise such as his bank would help build a prosperous society by offering equal economic opportunity and greater freedom for the masses. By providing easy and inexpensive credit, he—more than anyone else in his time—contributed to deliberately transforming and elevating the working class into a new expanded middle class.

He stood up proudly for what he believed in, thinking of his father who had lost his life in a dispute over one dollar. Saint Paul in the *Epistle to Timothy* (6:10) had clearly indicated the way: "The love of money is the root of all evil" meaning that it is not money *per se* that is the issue but the unconditional craving for it. When money becomes an end in itself, Giannini thought it could easily become "a yoke of servitude rather than a beacon of enlightenment."

He had the great distinction of helping to transform the society in which he lived. He saw himself as a defender of social and economic rights, assisting people to enjoy the benefits of free market trade in an honest way, defying every cliché. On several occasions he stated: "It has been my aim to distribute as much good as possible to make as many people as possible happy." He accomplished all of this by being a passionate doer and not a passive spectator. He was a true leader and one of the most enlightened and legendary protagonists of the twentieth century. With him, the American Dream became a reality, not just for the individual, but collectively, changing forever the social and economic landscape of his native California.

Notes

CHAPTER ONE: A CHALLENGING CHILDHOOD

1. Deanna Paoli Gumina, *The Italians of San Francisco 1850–1930*, (New York: Jerome S. Ozer Publishing, 1978).
2. Teresa De Martini to George Solari, February 9, 1947, Bank of America Archives (BAA).
3. *San Jose Mercury and Herald*, August 14, 1876, in Felice A. Bonadio, *A.P. Giannini Banker of America*, (Berkeley: University of California Press, 1994), p. 4.
4. John Leale, *Recollections of a Tule Sailor*, (San Francisco: G. Fields, 1939), p. 64.

CHAPTER TWO: LORENZO SCATENA: A NEW ROLE MODEL AT THE WATERFRONT

5. Dana Haight Cattani and Angela B. Haight, *A.P. Giannini: The Man with the Midas Touch*, (Bloomington, IN: Authorhouse, 2009), p. 5.
6. *San Francisco Chronicle*, February 27, 1927.
7. Giannini, interview with Walter Bruns, March 31, 1949, Bank of America Archives (BAA).
8. Ibid.
9. Gerald D. Nash, *A.P Giannini and the Bank of America*, (Norman: University of Oklahoma Press, 1992), p. 16.

10. Paul Rink, *Building the Bank of America*, (Chicago: Encyclopedia Britannica Press Inc., 1963), p. 31.

11. Nash, p. 17.

12. Ibid., p. 15.

13. Haight-Cattani and Haight, p. 10.

14. Giannini, interview with Walter Bruns, March 31, 1949, BAA.

15. Felice A. Bonadio, *A.P. Giannini: Banker of America*, (Berkeley: University of California Press, 1994), p. 11.

16. Nash, p. 16.

17. Julian Dana, *A.P. Giannini. Giant in the West: a Biography*, (New York: Prentice-Hall, 1947), p. 33–35.

18. Bonadio, p.16.

19. Ibid., p. 15.

20. Haight-Cattani and Haight, p.14.

21. Rink, p. 34.

22. Giannini, interview with Bessie James, October 7, 1947.

23. Bonadio, p. 21.

CHAPTER THREE: THE FOUNDING OF THE BANK OF ITALY

24. Rink, p. 42.

25. Giannini interview with Bessie James, September 26, 1947.

26. Interview with Marquis James and Bessie Rowland James, Bankamerica Corporation, 1954 and 1982, Washington.

27. Rink, p. 48.

28. Nash, p. 24.

29. Ibid., p. 27.

CHAPTER FOUR: THE EARTHQUAKE: DISASTER AND OPPORTUNITY

30. Rink, p. 51.

31. Haight-Cattani and Haight, p. 30.

32. Rink, p. 54.

33. Ibid., p. 53.

34. Dana, p. 53.

35. Haight-Cattani and Haight, p. 49.

36. Nash, p. 34.

37. *L'Italia*, "Facts and Figures Worthy of Consideration," April 18, 1916, translated by Dorothy Sturla, BAA.

38. Bonadio, p. 36.

39. Nash, p. 35.

40. Rink, p. 66.

41. Haight-Cattani and Haight, p. 52.

42. Ibid.

43. Rink, p. 65.

44. Ibid., p. 66.

CHAPTER FIVE: THE DAWN OF BRANCH BANKING

45. *San Francisco Chronicle*, August 17, 1908.

46. Rink, p. 69.

47. Dana, p. 57.

48. Ibid., p. 71.

49. Rink, p. 74.

50. Nash, p. 37.

51. Dana, p. 67.

52. Ibid., p. 68.

53. Rink, p. 86.

54. Haight-Cattani and Haight, p. 60.

55. Rink, p. 88.

56. APG to Attilio Giannini, August 14, 1936, BAA.

57. *San Francisco News*, March 19, 1928, BAA.

58. Haight-Cattani and Haight, p. 62.

59. Rink, p. 83.

60. Haight-Cattani and Haight, p. 60.

61. Dana, p. 73.

CHAPTER SIX: LOS ANGELES: AN OPPORTUNITY NOT TO BE MISSED

62. Nash, p. 45.

63. John Weaver, *Los Angeles: The Enormous Village, 1781–1981* (Santa Barbara: Capra Press, 1980).

64. Kevin Starr, *Material Dream: Southern California through the 1920s* (New York: Oxford University Press, 1990) p. 85.

65. Carey McWilliams, *Southern California Country* (New York: Duell, Sloan and Pearce, 1946) p.128–37.
66. Rink, p. 98.
67. The Security Trust and Saving, First National, German American Trust and Saving, Farmers and Merchants National, Los Angeles Trust and Saving, Citizens National, and The Merchants National: *Los Angeles Daily Tribune*, January 2, 1913.
68. *Pacific Rural Press*, December 23, 1916.
69. *Pacific Rural Press*, March 4, 1916.
70. Nash, p. 51.
71. Bank of Italy Ledgers for 1915–18 compiled by Roscoe Evans, BAA.
72. Rink, p. 113.
73. Bonadio, p. 65.
74. Frances Dinkelspiel, *Towers of Gold*, (New York: St. Martin's Press, 2008) p. 10–11.
75. Ibid., p. 119.

CHAPTER SEVEN: THE LARGEST BANK WEST OF CHICAGO

76. Haight-Cattani and Haight, p. 71.
77. Financial Report, June 30, 1924, BAA.
78. Ibid., p. 75.
79. Dana, p. 114.
80. Bonadio, p. 76–79.

CHAPTER EIGHT: CELEBRATING TWENTY YEARS OF TENACIOUS EXPANSION

81. Nash, p. 64.
82. Marquis James and Bessie R. James, *Biography of a Bank: The story of Bank of America NT & SA 1904–1953* (San Francisco: Bank of America Corporate Archives, 1982) p. 270.
83. James and James, p. 194 and 222.
84. *The San Francisco Examiner*, February 16, 1927.
85. Nash, p. 69.
86. Rink, p. 133.
87. James and James, p. 200.
88. *Forbes*, February 1928, BAA.

89. *San Francisco Examiner*, February 22, 1927.
90. James and James, p. 289.

CHAPTER NINE: FULFILLING DREAMS

91. *Literary Digest*, January 1929, BAA.
92. *The San Francisco Chronicle*, May 21, 1929.
93. *The California Monthly*, May 1929. Giovanni Gentile, the Minister of Education of Italy, in expressing his appreciation/approbation of the Chair voiced his sentiments in this statement: "The Italians of California by aiding to promote a knowledge of Italian culture in that University not only fulfill a noble duty towards their native land, but are also contributing to the healthy development of modern society."
94. John G. Fucilla, *The Teaching of Italian in the United States*, AATI, 1968.
95. David Puttnam with Neil Watson, *Movies and Money*, (New York: Alfred A. Knopf, 1998) p. 18 and p. 32.
96. Puttnam, p. 95–96.
97. Charles Chaplin, *My Autobiography*, (London: Melville House 1964) p. 18.
98. Janet Wasko, *Movies and Money: Financing the American Film Industry* (Norwood, N.J: Praeger 1982) p. 13.
99. Joseph Kennedy, *Story of the Films* (Cambridge, A.W. Shaw Co.1927) p. 78–79.
100. Puttnam, p. 96.
101. *San Francisco Examiner*, August 20, 1935.
102. Kennedy, p. 80–81.
103. Frank Taylor, "He is No Angel," *Saturday Evening Post*, January 14, 1939.
104. Nash, p. 96.
105. For these early cartoons see "The Big Bad Wolf," *Fortune*, November 1934.
106. "The Dream Merchant" (1901–1966), *New York Times*, December 16, 1966.
107. Kevin Starr, *Golden Gate*, (New York: Bloomsbury Press, 2010) p. 2.
108. Starr, p. 78–79.
109. Starr, p. 17.

CHAPTER TEN: NATIONWIDE BANKING: A LIFE-LONG MISSION

110. Dana, p.159–160.
111. *San Francisco Bulletin*, February 17, 1928.
112. James and James, p. 281.
113. Nash, p.103.
114. James and James, p. 278.
115. *Washington Evening Star*, May 10, 1928.
116. Bonadio, p. 137.
117. *The New York Times*, September 5, 1928.
118. *San Francisco Examiner*, September 11, 1928.
119. James and James, p. 291.
120. Bonadio, p. 143.
121. Ibid., p. 150.

CHAPTER ELEVEN: BETRAYAL FROM WITHIN

122. *The New York Times*, October 30, 1929.
123. *San Francisco Chronicle*, December 4, 1929.
124. *San Francisco Examiner*, March 29, 1929.
125. Bonadio, p.161 and *San Francisco Chronicle*, March 27, 1930.
126. Attilio Giannini to Mario Giannini, March 15, 1930, BAA.
127. *San Francisco Chronicle*, June 6, 1930; *Los Angeles Times*, July 12, 1930.
128. Claire Giannini Hoffman, interview with Felice A. Bonadio.
129. Bonadio, p. 172.
130. James and James, p. 313.
131. APG to Armando Pedrini, December 25, 1930, BAA.
132. *Time*, April 6, 1931.
133. Ibid., p. 313.
134. James and James, p. 318.
135. Bonadio, p. 178.

CHAPTER TWELVE: RETURN TO THE BATTLEFIELD

136. Dana, p. 202.
137. *Wall Street Journal*, September 23, 1931.
138. James and James, p. 329.
139. Dana, p. 209.
140. Haight-Cattani and Haight, p. 88.

141. James and James, p. 334.
142. Dana, p. 220.
143. *San Francisco Chronicle*, February 22, 1932.
144. *New York Times*, February 16, 1932.

CHAPTER THIRTEEN: BACK TO THE GOOD TIMES

145. *Wall Street Journal*, July 25, 1932.

CHAPTER FOURTEEN: UNDER SIEGE AGAIN

146. Bonadio, p. 204–205.
147. Dana, p. 237–238.
148. Nash, p.111.
149. *San Francisco Examiner*, October 23, 1934.
150. Dana, p. 256.
151. Dana, p. 250.

CHAPTER FIFTEEN: THE NEW HEART OF THE BANK OF AMERICA

152. Nash, p. 133–134.
153. Nash, p. 137.
154. *San Francisco Chronicle*, November 3, 1945.
155. *San Francisco Chronicle*, March 31, 1948.
156. Bonadio, p. 294.

CHAPTER SIXTEEN: GIANNINI'S LEGACY

157. *San Francisco Examiner, San Francisco Chronicle*, June 9, 1949.
158. *New York Times*, June 5, 1949.
159. *Los Angeles Times*, June 5,1949.

EPILOGUE

160. Yona Friedman, Utopie realizzabili, (Paris: Quodlibet, 2003), p. 36.

About the Author

A journalist and a cultural mediator, Dr. Francesca Valente was director of several Italian Cultural Institutes (IIC) in North America for over thirty years. In her most recent post in Los Angeles, she coordinated the eight IIC of USA and Canada. She produced several short films, edited over 100 catalogues and publications, and translated 35 works by such renowned authors as Margaret Atwood, Giorgio Bassani, Leonard Cohen, Northrop Frye, Marshall McLuhan, Michael Ondaatje, and Pier Paolo Pasolini. She has lectured at University of California at Berkeley; University of Southern California; LUISS University and La Sapienza, Rome.

The author would like to thank Michelle Tripodi for her committed assistance and hard work; Robert Barbera for offering her the opportunity to come to know one of the greatest Italian-Americans of the 20th century; Anne and Virginia Giannini for sharing so many interesting memories; Alessandro Baccari for enriching her with interesting anecdotes on A.P. Giannini's habits in North Beach; Laura Piccirillo Waste for sharing the vivid memory of Maria Teresa Piccirillo who founded the Chair of Italian Cultura at U. C. Berkeley; Barbara Spackman Cecchetti, Professor of Italian Studies, Department Chair of the University of California, Berkeley; Nancy Genn, artist, Berkeley, for her interest in the project and help; Amelia Antonucci for her kind assistance; and the San Francisco Public Library for their special collaboration.

NOW AVAILABLE FROM THE MENTORIS PROJECT

America's Forgotten Founding Father
A Novel Based on the Life of Filippo Mazzei
by Rosanne Welch

Christopher Columbus: His Life and Discoveries
by Mario Di Giovanni

Fermi's Gifts
A Novel Based on the Life of Enrico Fermi
by Kate Fuglei

God's Messenger
The Astounding Achievements of Mother Cabrini
A Novel Based on the Life of Mother Frances X. Cabrini
by Nicole Gregory

Harvesting the American Dream
A Novel Based on the Life of Ernest Gallo
by Karen Richardson

Marconi and His Muses
A Novel Based on the Life of Guglielmo Marconi
by Pamela Winfrey

Saving the Republic
A Novel Based on the Life of Marcus Cicero
by Eric D. Martin

Soldier, Diplomat, Archaeologist
A Novel Based on the Bold Life of Louis Palma di Cesnola
by Peg A. Lamphier

COMING SOON FROM THE MENTORIS PROJECT

A Novel Based on the Life of Alessandro Volta
A Novel Based on the Life of Amerigo Vespucci
A Novel Based on the Life of Andrea Palladio
A Novel Based on the Life of Angelo Dundee
A Novel Based on the Life of Antonin Scalia
A Novel Based on the Life of Antonio Meucci
A Novel Based on the Life of Buzzie Bavasi
A Novel Based on the Life of Cesare Becaria
A Novel Based on the Life of Federico Fellini
A Novel Based on the Life of Filippo Brunelleschi
A Novel Based on the Life of Frank Capra
A Novel Based on the Life of Galileo Galilei
A Novel Based on the Life of Giovanni Andrea Doria
A Novel Based on the Life of Giovanni di Bicci de' Medici
A Novel Based on the Life of Giuseppe Garibaldi
A Novel Based on the Life of Giuseppe Verdi
A Novel Based on the Life of Guido Monaco
A Novel Based on the Life of Harry Warren
A Novel Based on the Life of Henry Mancini
A Novel Based on the Life of John Cabot
A Novel Based on the Life of Judge John Sirica
A Novel Based on the Life of Lenonardo Covello
A Novel Based on the Life of Leonardo de Vinci
A Novel Based on the Life of Luca Pacioli
A Novel Based on the Life of Maria Montessori
A Novel Based on the Life of Mario Andretti
A Novel Based on the Life of Mario Cuomo
A Novel Based on the Life of Niccolo Machiavelli
A Novel Based on the Life of Peter Rodino
A Novel Based on the Life of Pietro Belluschi
A Novel Based on the Life of Publius Cornelius Scipio
A Novel Based on the Life of Robert Barbera
A Novel Based on the Life of Saint Augustine of Hippo
A Novel Based on the Life of Saint Francis of Assisi
A Novel Based on the Life of Saint Thomas Aquinas
A Novel Based on the Life of Vince Lombardi

For more information on these titles and
The Mentoris Project, please visit
www.mentorisproject.org.

Made in the USA
San Bernardino, CA
08 February 2018